GOOD BOSS,
BAD BOSS

Good Boss, Bad Boss

How to Be the Best...and Learn from the Worst

ROBERT I. SUTTON, PhD

BUSINESS PLUS

NEW YORK   BOSTON

Business Plus
Hachette Book Group
237 Park Avenue
New York, NY 10017
www.HachetteBookGroup.com

Business Plus is an imprint of Grand Central Publishing.
The Business Plus name and logo are trademarks of Hachette Book Group, Inc.

Printed in the United States of America

First Edition: September 2010

10 9 8 7 6 5 4 3 2 1

Library of Congress Cataloging-in-Publication Data

Sutton, Robert I.
   Good boss, bad boss: how to be the best...and learn from the worst / by Robert I. Sutton. —1st ed.
      p. cm.
   Includes index.
   ISBN 978-0-446-55608-8
   1. Supervision of employees.   2. Managing your boss.   I. Title.

HF5549.12.S88 2010
658.4'09—dc22

                                                                    2009053414

To Marina, for every sweet little thing

CONTENTS

GOOD BOSS,
BAD BOSS

PREFACE

From Assholes to Bosses

My last book, *The No Asshole Rule*, is about the damage done by workplace jerks, what it takes to survive a nasty workplace, and how organizations can screen out, reform, and expel these demeaning and destructive creeps. I was overwhelmed by the sheer volume of reactions to the book, and more so by the pain, fear, and desperate cries for help (and success stories, too) that I heard and responded to day after day. As a colleague put it, "Bob, you have become the asshole guy—it's a job that takes a lot of time and emotional energy." I was inundated with asshole stories from all over the world. Thousands of personal stories, survival tips, and new studies poured in via e-mail and comments on my blog, calls from complete strangers, and nearly every work-related conversation that I had—regardless of the advertised topic of a meeting, class, or speech. There was no escaping it outside of work either. People told me asshole stories everyplace I went: cocktail parties, family gatherings, soccer games, weddings, a bat mitzvah, a funeral, and even a parent-teacher conference.

The deluge has slowed but not stopped. Consider a recent week. I received and answered nineteen "asshole" e-mails, including those from a police sergeant in New York, a Starbuck's barista in Chicago, an accountant from Italy, and an HR manager from Wisconsin who struggled to implement the no asshole rule in a small company (her old boss loved it, but her new boss is a screamer and thinks it is a dumb idea). I talked with a Hollywood insider about the asshole-management methods used by people who work with Academy Award–winning producer Scott Rudin—who is infamous for his tirades, tantrums, and burning through as many as fifty assistants a year. One tip for dealing with Rudin was "He hates when you look at him; avoid it or you are asking for it." This advice was offered in concert with a (possibly mythical but often-repeated) story that Rudin had dumped an assistant on the side of a Los Angeles freeway as punishment for glancing at him in the rearview mirror too many times. That same week, I spent most of a ninety-minute interview with a Japanese journalist listening to bitter complaints about his temperamental, unfair, and incompetent boss back in Tokyo.

This deluge revealed new twists about how assholes do their dirty work and how to battle back against these creeps. Adamant and enthusiastic readers bombarded me with topics they wanted covered in a sequel to *The No Asshole Rule*. An Australian consultant asked for tips about dealing with asshole clients. A New Jersey schoolteacher requested tactics for battling subtle, or "camouflaged," assholes. A Catholic priest wanted tactics for dealing with difficult parishioners. During one of my speeches, a pushy audience member insisted that I drop my other projects and devote my life to leading an "anti-asshole movement." People in the book business pressed for a sequel, too. My favorite inquiry came in a handwritten note from Marie-Pierre Vaslet, who edited the French translation of *The No Asshole Rule* (*Objectif Zéro-Sale-Con*). In her elegant cursive, Marie-Pierre seemed to be asking, "Bob, will I be seeing *The Asshole Shits Again* soon?"

These pressures and temptations provoked me to start working on a sequel. But a funny thing happened along the way. As I thought about all those stories and conversations, and read pertinent research, I realized "the asshole problem" wasn't an isolated concern for most employees and in most workplaces. It was intertwined with feelings, opinions, and aspirations that swirled around a central figure: THE BOSS. I realized that the best bosses did far more than enforce the no asshole rule. They took diverse and intertwined steps to create effective and humane workplaces. And the worst bosses weren't just guilty of letting assholes rule the roost. Their incompetence reared its ugly head in a host of other ways.

Bosses were the central figures in most stories I heard about the creeps who damaged employees' performance and self-worth. Consider the salesman whose e-mail was titled, "Had leukemia, bullied by a bad manager." When chemotherapy began draining his energy, his wicked boss doubled his sales quota and called each day to berate him for being "a wimp" and "a fuckup." Or the legal secretary who was treated as if she were invisible by the attorneys she served. These pompous and self-absorbed jerks never greeted her when passing by and often held long and loud conversations right in front of her desk—without stopping for a moment to acknowledge her existence. Or the obstetrician who was belittled so brutally by senior physicians during her training that it undermined her confidence during difficult deliveries throughout her career.

The prevalence of asshole bosses is confirmed by careful studies. A 2007 Zogby survey of nearly eight thousand American adults found that, of those abused by workplace bullies (37% of respondents), 72% were bullied by superiors. Stories about the damage done by bully bosses are bolstered by systematic research. University of Florida researchers found that employees with abusive bosses were more likely than others to slow down or make errors on purpose (30% vs. 6%), hide from their bosses (27% vs. 4%), not put in maximum effort (33% vs. 9%), and take sick time when they weren't sick (29% vs. 4%). Abused employees were three times *less* likely to make suggestions or go out of their way to fix workplace problems. Abusive superiors also drive out employees: over 20 million Americans have left jobs to flee from workplace bullies, most of whom were bosses.

Yet when people look for (or dream of) a great boss, they want more than someone who just isn't a certified asshole. They want a civilized boss who does many things well. Take the young professor who told me about her escape from a nasty and sexist department chairman. She landed a job with a new chair who was not just a delightful human being; he was renowned for getting resources for faculty and protecting them from petty and time-consuming political battles.

The No Asshole Rule touched a nerve in bosses (and would-be bosses) because treating people with dignity is something that skilled bosses do—but not the only thing. I think of the high school principal from Illinois who worked to get her teachers to "stop trying to destroy each other because you will be better for it and so will our students." Changing the emotional tone of the place was part of a five-point plan she was implementing to turn around a troubled school.

I think of the chief surgeon who treats nurses and residents with respect because, during his own surgical residency, he vowed not to become a demeaning and self-absorbed creep like the surgeons who trained him. He emphasized that respect was important for reducing medical mistakes because nurses and residents need to feel safe—even obligated—to point out errors made by him and other senior physicians without fear of retribution. As another physician explained, just because you aren't an asshole doesn't mean that a nurse will feel comfortable pointing out that you screwed up. The best bosses don't see the no asshole rule as an isolated path to excellence. They see it as part of a bigger tool kit.

In short, workplace assholes led me to write *Good Boss,*

Bad Boss because I was inundated with so many people who yearned to be skilled bosses and to work for one.

I use the word *boss* rather than *leader, manager,* or *supervisor* (although all are bosses) because it implies an authority figure that has direct and frequent contact with subordinates—and who is responsible for personally directing and evaluating their work. This book is not about what it takes to set the strategy for a large enterprise or lead hundreds or thousands of underlings (most of whom a leader barely knows or has never met). Whether you are the CEO of a Fortune 500 company, a head chef, or a basketball coach, manage a Starbucks, or lead a product development team, your success depends on the nitty-gritty of dealing with the people you work with most closely, who see you in action up close, and you are expected to personally guide, inspire, and discipline. When people talk about "my boss," it conjures up the sounds of people's voices and facial expressions, images of all-too-human relationships where people know too much about each other's quirks, foibles, and habits—even if much of that contact occurs via phone calls, e-mails, text messages, or video conferences rather than face-to-face. Being a boss or having a boss is about dealing with the confidence, comfort, warmth, resentment, confusion, and flashes of anger and despair that pervade any relationship where one person wields power in an up-close and personal way over another.

Good Boss, Bad Boss is about what the best bosses do, not the ordinary or barely competent ones. Most people don't want to settle for being (or having) a mediocre boss.

People like that professor who wrote me about their successful escapes from asshole bosses searched for great bosses—not just adequate ones. My wife, Marina Park, was especially insistent that I write about what the best bosses do. Marina has been a boss for a long time. She spent eight years as managing partner of a law firm before switching to the nonprofit sector. Now she is CEO of the Girl Scouts of Northern California. When I told Marina about this book, her reaction was intense and immediate: "I want to be a great boss. I want to know what that looks like. That is the book I want to read."

The upshot, as Marina would have it, is that this book focuses on what the best bosses do. My conclusions and advice about the actions of the best (and worst) bosses are based on what I've learned from a huge pile of academic studies during my thirty-year career as a researcher and from thousands of observations and conversations with bosses (and their colleagues) from workplaces of all kinds. The evidence-based advice here is also shaped by my biases and values about what the best bosses say and do. In particular, I don't care if you lead the most productive salespeople in your organization, coach a world championship soccer team, or are principal of an award-winning high school; if you treat your people like dirt, you don't deserve to be called a great boss in my book.

Good Boss, Bad Boss focuses on the differences between the best and worst bosses. I contrast the best and worst moves that they make when performing essential chores like taking charge, making wise decisions, turning talk into action, and doing their dirty work. Most of the research introduced here compares "better versus worse" actions that bosses take. I do so because the nuances and impact of doing the right thing become crystal clear when placed alongside the wrong thing. If you are a boss, you can save yourself much grief by considering the screwups and setbacks of fellow bosses. As former U.S. First Lady Eleanor Roosevelt is credited with saying, "Learn from the mistakes of others. You can't live long enough to make them all yourself."

The cautionary tales in *Good Boss, Bad Boss* not only can save time and money, they can spare you humiliation. Chapter 7 shows there are times when you need to "keep your big mouth shut." I describe a partner and head of the securities practice at a large law firm who talked loudly about upcoming layoffs on his cell phone as he rode in a crowded train—and named approximately twenty attorneys slated to lose their jobs. His bellowing was overheard by a fellow passenger, who figured out the partner's firm, his name, and that he was speaking with the COO. This anonymous passenger then wrote a blog post about the conversation. Embarrassed firm leaders apologized for their indiscreet partner and admitted that, yes, layoffs were coming soon. That loud partner learned his lesson; but it is a lot easier to *learn from* that guy than to *be* that guy.

If you are serious about becoming a skilled and compassionate boss, just reading this or any other book isn't enough. Greatness comes only through dogged effort, doing many small things well, getting up after each hard knock, and helping your people press forward at every turn. The best bosses don't ride into town, save the day with a bold move or two, declare victory, and then rest on their laurels. There is no final victory. The main reward for success is usually that you get to keep doing a damn hard (but often satisfying) job for a while longer. Despite the horseshit spewed out by too many management gurus, there are no magic bullets, instant cures, or easy shortcuts to becoming a great boss. Anyone who tells you otherwise is a liar. The best bosses succeed because they keep chipping away at a huge pile of dull, interesting, fun, rewarding, trivial, frustrating, and often ridiculous chores. That's why this book is called *Good Boss, Bad Boss*. Devoting relentless attention to doing one good thing after another—however small—is the only path I know to becoming and remaining a great boss.

I wish I could promise you that the path was easier. Yet there are stark differences between what superb and lousy bosses do, differences backed by piles of rigorous studies. *Good Boss, Bad Boss* blends this research with true stories to reveal the mindset, measure, and actions of the best bosses—along with lessons gleaned from mistakes that even the best bosses sometimes make and the worst make again and again.

SECTION I

Setting the Stage

CHAPTER 1

The Right Mindset

Bosses matter. Bosses matter because most employees have bosses, are bosses, or play both roles. There are at least 21 million bosses in the United States, with estimates running as high as 38 million. Over 90 percent of U.S. employees have at least one boss, someone who presides over them in the local hierarchy. Bosses work in over fifty occupations, from top executives to military officers, to ship captains, to head cooks, to funeral directors. Bosses matter to everyone they oversee. But they matter most to immediate followers, those just beneath them in the local pecking order, who bosses guide and evaluate at close range, and who tangle with their virtues, foibles, and quirks day after day. The success or failure of every boss hinges on how well or how badly he or she navigates these vexing and all-too-human relationships.

Early in my career, I saw the difference a boss can make when my friend Corey Billington went to work for

Hewlett-Packard. Corey joined the SPaM group, which un-covers and invents ways to improve HP's supply chains. The group leader (I'll call him Hector) wowed executives with big ideas and flashy presentations. Unfortunately, Hector spent hardly any time talking to his people and showed little interest in their work or careers. Hector ignored his team for long stretches and then—at seemingly random intervals—rushed in and demanded that everyone work on some urgent project. To paraphrase one SPaM member, "Every now and then, he would ride in on his white horse, lead a charge, kill the enemy, declare victory, and gallop away. Then we wouldn't see him for a while." People at SPaM got fed up with Hector's antics and gave him low marks on the employee attitude survey. To man-agement's credit, they moved Hector to another job and made Corey the boss.

Corey used a different style. He listened to his people, worked with them to uncover their skills and hopes, and labored to land projects they would enjoy and would bol-ster SPaM's reputation. The first years were tough. SPaM had trouble getting good work, an early project failed, Corey made a hiring mistake, and some executives ques-tioned whether HP needed SPaM at all. But Corey per-sisted, helping his people develop new skills, learn from setbacks, and grow a group of loyal clients inside and—eventually—outside HP. Under Hector, SPaM's consultants were paid much less than people who did similar work elsewhere and he made no effort to raise their pay. Corey fought for them, because "not getting paid based on our value sucked. I had to create a job family for my organization, which was no small amount of work." Life slowly got better at SPaM. Within five years, they were doing high-profile work and were named "the best strategy group" by INFORMS (a prestigious academic society)—and about 15 percent of their work was done at "remarkably high rates" for clients outside HP.

Bosses Matter

The punch line of the SPaM story—that the difference between a bad boss and a good boss matters a lot—is bolstered by a pile of studies. For starters, having a good boss decreases your chances of getting a heart attack. A Swedish study that followed 3,122 men for ten years found that those with the best bosses (e.g., who were considerate, specified clear goals, and got changes implemented) suffered fewer heart attacks than those with bad bosses. Co-author Anna Nyberg reported, "If you have a good boss, you have at least a 20 percent lower risk and if you stay with your boss for four years, you have at least a 39 percent lower risk." This 2008 study fits a long-standing pattern. Researcher Robert Hogan found that whether a study was done in "1948, 1958, 1968, 1998," in "London, Baltimore, Seattle, Honolulu," among "postal workers, milk truck drivers, school teachers," the results are pretty much identical: about 75 percent of the workforce reports that their immediate supervisor is the most stressful part of their job.

Bosses make the biggest difference when they wield direct and personal influence over followers, such as in teams and small organizations. To illustrate, Robert Keller examined 118 leaders of small (four- or five-person) project teams. Teams with stronger leaders (e.g., charismatic, intellectually stimulating, and set clear expectations) did better work, cranked it out faster, and were more cost-efficient. Keller's five-year follow-up also showed that better bosses led teams that designed more profitable products and got them to market faster. Keller's findings ring true to me. In the 1990s, my doctoral students and I observed numerous product development teams in action. The differences between the best- and the worst-led teams were striking. One team (at a now-defunct organization) spent six months talking and talking about what products to develop, and the boss discouraged members from drawing—let alone building—prototypes. She rewarded smart talk, not smart action. This poorly led team never developed a single prototype, even though my student following the team (an experienced product designer) believed he could build a working prototype of the gizmo the team was imagining in just a few hours. In contrast, a well-led team we studied elsewhere built a promising prototype during the first week of a project—which they assembled in about thirty minutes, right after generating the idea.

Sports teams are another setting where bosses work elbow to elbow with followers, and so it is not surprising that managing and coaching skills propel performance. Lawrence Kahn's eighteen-year study of major league baseball teams shows that the best managers (with better win-loss records and more major league experience) consistently inspired both hitters and pitchers to perform above their career averages; in contrast, the worst managers stymied players so they performed below their career averages. Similarly, studies of National Basketball Association teams show that coaches with strong track records have pronounced positive effects on performance—an effect evident during their first year on the job. Basketball coaches can wield direct and timely influence because only five players are on the court at once and they can choreograph plays (and emotions they express to players) as the action unfolds just a few feet from where they sit or stand during games.

Bosses mattered massively in studies conducted by Gallup's army of researchers over the past thirty years. Gallup's surveys of over 100,000 employees in more than 2,500 diverse businesses show that "managers trump companies." Employees' immediate bosses have far more impact on engagement and performance than whether their companies are rated as great or lousy places to work. Related research shows that good bosses are especially crucial to employee performance in otherwise lousy workplaces. As leadership researcher Robert Hogan concludes from numerous careful studies, including the Gallup surveys, "people do not quit organizations, they quit bad bosses." A 2007 Gallup survey of U.S. employees revealed that 24 percent would fire their boss if given the chance. Gallup concludes that crummy bosses are a primary reason that 56 percent of employees are "checked-out" and "sleepwalking through their days." Worse yet, the most bitter employees (the "actively disengaged" 18 percent) undermine their coworkers' accomplishments. Gallup has also found sweeping differences between organizations that have many great bosses versus many crummy bosses. In businesses where a higher proportion of employees report that their immediate bosses care about them, employee satisfaction, retention, and productivity are higher, and so is profitability.

Yet the leader of an organization still matters more than the other bosses. The top dog sets the tone for how his or her direct reports behave—which reverberates through the system. I worked with a large company where the CEO did almost all the talking in meetings, interrupted anyone who tried to get in a word edgewise, and aggressively silenced any underling who voiced a dissenting view. The executive vice presidents on his senior team complained bitterly (behind his back, of course) about the antics of their bossy boss. But I noticed that as soon as the CEO left the room, the most powerful EVP started acting exactly like his boss. Then, when that EVP departed, the next highest-ranking boss remaining in the room began mimicking the CEO's overbearing style. It was fascinating to watch this behavior travel down the local pecking order.

The ways that senior leaders treat direct reports create numerous other ripple effects that travel down and across the hierarchy, shaping a company's culture and performance. A study of sixty-six of the fastest growing new

U.S. firms showed that the best CEOs blended a "top-down" directive approach with a more participative "shared leadership" approach in managing their top teams. This research showed that when CEOs used this one-two punch of directive and participative approaches to lead senior teams, their companies enjoyed superior performance—growing both revenue and numbers of personnel faster than similar firms. Other research confirms that how CEOs manage their top teams trigger reactions that affect the entire organization. For example, when CEOs are given (or seize) far more pay and power than their direct reports, such gaps are linked to weaker company performance—perhaps because domineering CEOs are prone to hubris, and their comparatively powerless underlings can't stop their overbearing bosses from ramming through bad decisions.

Related research shows that when the CEO encourages other top team members to engage in constructive conflict, better decisions are made, which in turn fuels superior organizational performance. The same message emerges from historian Doris Kearns Goodwin's best seller *Team of Rivals: The Political Genius of Abraham Lincoln.* Lincoln had the courage to place three of his toughest opponents and critics in his cabinet after winning the 1860 election: William Seward, Salmon Chase, and Edward Bates. Goodwin documents how Lincoln exercised the skills to soothe their massive egos, encourage constructive conflict, and foment cooperation among these and other strong-willed followers in ways that not only created effective team dynamics but, more crucially, generated decisions that benefitted the nation and helped keep it intact during the U.S. Civil War. Even in the largest organization or institution, how the boss at the top of the pecking order treats direct reports spawns ripple effects that can influence the system's ultimate success or failure.

The upshot of these and so many other studies and stories is that bosses pack a wallop, especially on their direct reports. Bosses shape how people spend their days and whether they experience joy or despair, perform well or badly, or are healthy or sick. Unfortunately, there are hoards of mediocre and downright rotten bosses out there, and big gaps between the best and the worst. Watch and talk to people who answer to multiple bosses: you will see how the same employee doing the same work reacts to good and bad leaders. In the spring of 2009, I was waiting in line at my local Safeway to buy groceries. A check-out clerk got on the microphone and announced a five-minute Easter Seals fund-raising drive was starting; she encouraged donations for children with autism and other disabilities. This clerk also announced to the entire store that she was making this plea as a favor to Dave, her manager. When it was my turn to check out, as I handed her my donation, she said, "I hate most managers; I wouldn't do a thing for them. But I love Dave and I will do whatever he asks." I ran back to my car and wrote down her words because, for me, they brought the research to life: when she worked for Dave, she was delighted to do extra work, and her enthusiasm infected colleagues and customers.

When she worked for a boss she hated, all that extra effort and good cheer evaporated.

The gaps revealed by these studies and stories persist even though most bosses want to be great and most employees want wonderful bosses, which raises the question: *If you are a boss who wants to do great work, what can you do about it?* Good Boss, Bad Boss is devoted to answering that question. This chapter shows how the best bosses think. If you are a boss, the beliefs and assumptions you hold about yourself, your work, and your people shape what you do every day and how you (and others) judge if things are going well or badly. The best bosses embrace five beliefs that are stepping stones to effective action.

1. Don't Crush the Bird

Tommy Lasorda has served the Los Angeles Dodgers baseball team as a player, a coach, or an executive since 1949, including a twenty-year stint as manager. Lasorda once said, "I believe that managing is like holding a dove in your hand. If you hold it too tightly, you kill it, but if you hold it too loosely, you lose it." I call this Lasorda's Law, as it captures the delicate balance that every good boss seeks between managing too much and too little.

Researchers Daniel Ames and Frank Flynn proposed a hypothesis reminiscent of Lasorda's Law: managers who are too assertive will damage relationships with superiors, peers, and followers; but managers who are not assertive enough won't press followers to achieve sufficiently tough goals. So Ames and Flynn speculated that the best bosses would be rated roughly average on terms like *competitive, aggressive, passive,* and *submissive* by followers. They asked 213 MBA students to rate their most recent boss's assertiveness. As predicted, moderately assertive bosses were rated as most effective overall, most likely to succeed in the future, and as someone the MBAs would work with again. Ames and Flynn imply that a sign of a "perfectly assertive" boss is that followers may *notice that they don't notice* their boss's aggressiveness, competitiveness, passiveness, and submissiveness:

> Like salt in a sauce, too much overwhelms the dish; too little is similarly distracting; but just the right amount allows the other flavors to dominate our experience. Just as food is rarely praised for being perfectly salted, leaders may somewhat infrequently be praised for being perfectly assertive.

Effective bosses know it is sometimes best to leave their people alone. They realize that keeping a close eye on people often either has no effect on performance or undermines it—in contrast to micromanagers, who believe their relentless attention and advice bolsters performance. Experiments at Stanford show that when bosses scrutinized and coached underlings closely, many believed they improved performance, even when it was *impossible* for those bosses to affect their subordinates' performance.

So you may believe that watching your people closely is helping, but this research suggests you could be living in a fool's paradise. Nosy bosses also undermine performance by asking annoying and useless questions that interrupt people's work. And followers who are closely monitored become less creative because—to avoid screwing up in front of the boss—they stick to tried-and-true paths.

The best management is sometimes less management or no management at all. William Coyne, who led 3M's Research and Development efforts for over a decade, believed a big part of his job was to leave his people alone and protect them from other curious executives. As he put it: "After you plant a seed in the ground, you don't dig it up every week to see how it is doing."

Yet, as Lasorda's Law and Ames and Flynn's research suggest, good bosses don't just ignore their people or shower them with unconditional warm fuzziness. There are times when bosses need to coach people, discipline, communicate direction, and interject in hundreds of other little ways. Renowned theatrical director Frank Hauser offered lovely advice about walking this line. He was talking about directing plays, but his wisdom applies to other bosses: "You are not the parent of this child we call the play. You are present at its birth for *clinical* reasons, like a doctor or a midwife. Your job most of the time is to simply do no harm. When something goes wrong, however, your awareness that something is awry—and your clinical intervention to correct it—can determine whether the child will live or die."

Like Frank Hauser, savvy bosses travel through their days in search of the sweet spot between interjecting too little and too much, keeping a close eye on when more or less pressure, nagging, and intimidation is needed to get the best out of their people (and for provoking respect and dignity rather than contempt).

2. Grit Gets You There

The best bosses think and act like they are running a marathon, not a sprint. Hector at HP failed because he saw his job as riding in to lead a dramatic victory now and then, and little else. Corey succeeded by taking the long view, by grinding it out day after day. Researchers use the word *grit* to describe this mindset, which Professor Angela Duckworth and her colleagues define as "perseverance and passion toward long-term goals." They add, "Grit entails working strenuously toward challenges, maintaining effort and interest despite failure, adversity, and plateaus in progress. The gritty individual approaches achievement as a marathon, his or her advantage is stamina." Albert Einstein saw himself as gritty rather than brilliant and allegedly said, "It's not that I am so smart, it is just that I stay with my problems longer."

Great bosses instill grit in followers. They are dogged and patient, pressing themselves and others to move ever forward. Gritty bosses create urgency without treating life as one long emergency.

Glenn Osaka has grit. He was hired in 2000 to be the

CEO of Reactivity, a high-flying Silicon Valley start-up. Reactivity consulted on technically difficult aspects of building websites and incubated new companies. In early 2001, they were flush with earnings, stock from other start-ups, and millions in venture capital dollars. Then the bubble burst and Reactivity's income evaporated. Glenn and his team didn't give up and shut down, like most dot-coms did. They did a "major reset" in 2002, cutting back from seventy to thirteen people and returning 12 million dollars to investors. Glenn pushed and stirred people to brainstorm new business models to save the company. When they decided to become an enterprise software firm focused on security, Glenn pressed his team to build new products, hire the right people, and find customers. Glenn insisted they avoid detours and distractions. I watched Glenn persuade a software designer to stop consulting because, although it brought in money, Reactivity's survival hinged on building and selling the new product and little else. As John Lilly, chief technology officer and cofounder, told me, "Everyone who stayed through the transition did selling work, including making cold calls and talking with customers. That was a hard thing for a lot of engineers." Glenn's perseverance paid off. Reactivity acquired key customers, secured new financing, and was bought by Cisco for 135 million dollars in 2007.

Gritty bosses are driven by the nagging conviction that everything they and their people do could be better if they tried just a little harder or were just a bit more creative. Pixar's Brad Bird won Oscars for directing *The Incredibles* and *Ratatouille*. When my colleagues and I interviewed him in 2008, Bird kept talking about this "relentless restlessness." Bird had worked at Walt Disney's animation studio as a young man, and saw that the master animators who created classics like *Pinocchio, Fantasia, Dumbo*, and *Cinderella* were never satisfied: "They would get to the end of a film and they would say, 'I just started to feel like I understood the character, and I want to go back and do the whole thing over, because now I understand it, and the film's over.'" The studio went into decline after Walt Disney died, and the old masters' hungriness was replaced with complacency. Bird lamented that one new studio boss "had us all sit on the floor while he stood" and announced, "I'm satisfied with what I do." Bird was not impressed: "He lost me because I had already been with the guys whose worst stuff was 1,000 times better than this guy, and they were never satisfied with what they did." Bird's disgust led him to rock the Disney boat enough to get fired. The "relentless restlessness" that Bird picked up from those masters has served as rocket fuel throughout his career as a creator and director of animated films and TV shows, including *The Simpsons*.

This nagging conviction that nothing is ever quite good enough, that you can never stop learning and can never ever rest on your laurels isn't just a hallmark of skilled bosses in flashy industries. You see it in effective bosses like Jeanne Hammontree, who operates a Chick-Fil-A restaurant. Jeanne constantly experiments with ways to drive business to her place in the Coolsprings Galleria food court near Nashville, Tennessee: putting advertisements in elevators, dressing employees in a Chick-Fil-A cow suit (the company mascot) and sending them to other stores to take pictures with employees (who make up 50 percent of her customers), and strolling around the mall to introduce herself to store owners and employees. Jeanne's telltale stamina and relentlessness help explain why sales at her restaurant were up over 10 percent in 2008, a tough year for most Galleria businesses because of the economic downturn.

3. Small Wins Are the Path

Having long-term goals, and doggedly working toward them day after day, is a hallmark of bosses with grit. Great big goals set direction and energize people, but if goals are all you've got, you are doomed. The path to success is paved with small wins. Even the grandest and most glorious victories rest on a string of modest but constructive steps forward.

As a boss, framing what you and your people do as a series of manageable steps leads to better decisions, sustains motivation, and helps people experience less distress. Karl Weick, author of the classic article "Small Wins," shows that when a challenge is construed as too big, too complex, or too difficult, people freak out and freeze up. Weick shows that people think and act more effectively when they face and can conquer more modest and controllable challenges. Every gritty boss I discussed so far used a small-wins strategy. Corey Billington and Glenn Osaka each started with the goal of getting one paying customer. Brad Bird leads rollicking arguments about one tiny detail of a film after another. Jeanne Hammontree's success rests on tiny victories like digging a discount coupon out of the trash for a mom or meeting a new Sears employee as she strolls through the mall.

The best bosses realize that when they focus on the little things, the big things take care of themselves. Consider Andy Papathanassiou of Hendrick Motorsports. Hendrick fields four competitive racing teams for thirty-six events during each ten-month NASCAR season. Their drivers include four-time season champion Jimmie Johnson and past champions Jeff Gordon and Dale Earnhardt Jr. Andy oversees the recruiting and training of Hendrick's pit crews. Cars stop for gas and new tires six to twelve times during a typical 400- or 500-mile race. Winning is impossible without fast and consistent pit stops. If, say, a car must return to the pits because the lug nuts weren't tightened enough, the extra stop destroys a car's chances of winning that day. Skilled crews consistently complete pit stops in about thirteen seconds. Each tenth of a second matters because the gap between winners and losers is so tiny. The margin of victory was less than one second in over half the races during the 2007 season. At the Daytona Raceway, winner Jamie McMurray edged out Kyle Busch by less than 1/100th of a second.

Andy had no racing experience when he started working on pit crews. As a former Stanford football player, he was surprised that most crews didn't practice and even the best made numerous errors. Andy viewed a pit stop as much like executing a football play, so he organized crews to practice and worked with them to perfect tiny details. The teams that Andy led and coached—and his competitors, too—started discovering many little ways to speed up stops, like coiling the air hose in a figure-eight rather than a circle because it uncoiled more reliably. Andy also focused on finding athletically minded crewmen and giving them rigorous training. These small wins, along with thousands more in car design and driving technique, have enabled Hendrick to become the most consistent winner in the business.

The best bosses break down problems into bite-sized pieces and talk and act like each little task is something that people can complete without great difficulty. Doing so instills calmness and confidence, and spurs constructive action. One CEO I know used this strategy at a kick-off meeting for a big sales campaign. He led a discussion of the actions required to make the campaign a big success. The result was a to-do list with over one hundred tasks, which led people to worry aloud that accomplishing it all in a few months felt impossible. This boss reduced the group's angst by asking them to sort the list into "hard" and "easy" tasks. For each easy task, he asked who could do it and when they could get it done. Within fifteen minutes, the group realized that they could accomplish over half the tasks in just a few days. This lowered their anxiety, set the stage for a bunch of quick wins, and gave them confidence about the entire campaign.

4. Beware the Toxic Tandem

A few years ago, I did a workshop with a management team that was suffering from group dynamics problems. In particular, team members felt their boss, a senior vice president, was overbearing, listened poorly, and routinely ran over others. The VP denied all this and called his people "thin-skinned wimps."

I asked the team—the boss and five direct reports—to do a variation of an exercise I've used in the classroom for years. They spent about twenty minutes brainstorming ideas about products their business might bring to market; they then spent ten minutes narrowing their choices to just three: the most feasible, wildest, and most likely to fail. But as the group brainstormed and made these decisions, I didn't pay attention to the content of their ideas. Instead, I worked with a couple others from the company to make rough counts of the number of comments made by each member, the number of times each interrupted other members, and the number of times each was interrupted. During this short exercise, the VP made about 65 percent of the comments, interrupted others at least twenty times, and was never interrupted once. I then had the VP leave the room after the exercise and asked his five underlings to estimate the results; their recollections were quite accurate, especially about their boss's stifling actions. When we brought the VP back in, he recalled making about 25 percent of the comments, interrupting others two or three times, and being interrupted three or four times. When we gave the boss the results and told him that his direct reports made far more accurate estimates, he was flabbergasted and a bit pissed off at everyone in the room.

As this VP discovered, being a boss is much like being a high-status primate in any group: the creatures beneath you in the pecking order watch every move you make—and so they know a lot more about you than you know about them. Anthropologists who study chimpanzees, gorillas, and baboons report "followers look at the leader; the opposite does not happen as regularly or intensely." Studies of baboon troops show that a typical member glances at the alpha male every twenty or thirty seconds. Psychologist Susan Fiske observes, "Attention is directed *up* the hierarchy. Secretaries know more about their bosses than vice versa; graduate students know more about their advisors than vice versa." Fiske explains this happens because, like our fellow primates, "people pay attention to those who control their outcomes. In an effort to predict and possibly influence what is going to happen to them, people gather information about those with power."

Kelley Eskridge, managing partner of the training firm Humans at Work, wrote a wonderful description of how such scrutiny happens. She titled it "They watch everything you do."

If you get up from your desk, people watch to see where you're going. Someone always knows when you're in the bathroom. They watch your face when the VP of Production leaves your office, and make guesses about what your expression means. They watch to see if you smile more at Sally than you do at Tom, and make guesses about what that means too. They learn to read your tells—the way you drum your fingers when you're impatient, or the eyebrow you raise just before you cut off someone's explanation. They talk about your behavior when you're not around, and they assign meaning to everything.

You are constantly on your team's radar. They hear and see *everything* you do.

Eskridge adds: "Does that make you nervous? How about letting it make you *aware* instead?"

Linda Hudson, now a president at BAE Systems, learned this lesson when she became the first female president of General Dynamics. After landing the job, Hudson bought some fancy new suits, and a "lady at Nordstrom's had showed me how to tie a scarf in a very unusual kind of way for my new suit." She wore this outfit on her first day on the job, and to her amazement, "I come back to work the next day, and I run into no fewer than a dozen women in the organization who have on scarves tied exactly like mine." This incident helped Hudson gain the awareness that Eskridge suggests: "I realized that life was never going to be the way it had been before, that people were watching everything I did. And it wasn't just going to be about how I dressed. It was about my behavior, the example I set, the tone I set, the way I carried myself, how confident I was—all those kinds of things."

Unfortunately, unlike Linda Hudson, too many bosses become accustomed to such scrutiny and start talking and acting as if they are oblivious to it. This was certainly part of the problem with the VP who was unaware of his own behavior and of how closely his direct reports were watching it. And recall the legal secretary I mentioned in the preface, who suffered as the attorneys she served engaged in loud conversations right in front of her desk and acted as if she were invisible. People in power tend to become self-centered and oblivious to what their followers need, do, and say. That alone is bad enough. But the problem is compounded because a boss's self-absorbed words and deeds are usually scrutinized so closely by subordinates. I call this *the toxic tandem.*

To appreciate how such power poisoning plays out for bosses, consider the "cookie experiment" reported by psychologist Dacher Keltner and his colleagues. Three-person student teams were instructed to produce a short policy paper. Two members were randomly assigned to write it; the third member evaluated it and determined how much to pay the two "workers." After about thirty minutes, the experimenter brought in a plate of five cookies. It turned out that a little taste of power turned people into pigs: not only did the "bosses" tend to take a second cookie, they also displayed other symptoms of "disinhibited eating," chewing with their mouths open and scattering crumbs.

The cookie experiment illustrates a finding repeated in

many studies. When people (regardless of personality) wield power, their ability to lord it over others causes them to (1) become more focused on their own needs and wants; (2) become less focused on others' needs, wants, and actions; and (3) act as if written and unwritten rules others are expected to follow don't apply to them. Good bosses constantly guard against falling prey to the toxic tandem. As Kelley Eskridge advises, they never forget how closely their followers watch them, and they resist the urge to grab all the goodies for themselves and ignore their followers' feelings and needs. The advice that David Packard of HP fame gave to managers in 1958 applies just as well today: "Watch your smile, your tone of voice, the way you look at people, the way you greet them, the use of nicknames, a memory for faces, names and dates. These small things will refine your ability to get on with others." As Packard realized, your charges scrutinize even your most trivial and innocent actions, and their reactions shape how much of themselves they will dedicate to you and to their work.

5. Got Their Backs

Donovan Campbell led the "Joker One" Marine platoon in Ramadi during some of the bloodiest street battles of the Iraq war. Lieutenant Campbell devoted enormous effort to protecting his men, through little things like ordering them to rehearse over and over so they could get in and out of a Humvee quickly, and nagging them to eat and "push" water. And through big things, like when he believed his men were unnecessarily put in harm's way by a superior's decision, he argued back vehemently—although he couldn't always change their minds. One of the worst days of Campbell's life came after his platoon was ordered to take his executive officer (the "XO") to inspect construction work the U.S. government was paying for at a local school. Campbell resisted because it was in a dangerous area, and he had learned the hard way that waiting in the open with a bunch of marines and vehicles was an invitation for an insurgent attack. Campbell was overruled, but he insisted that the XO spend no more than ten minutes in the schoolhouse—preferably five—because the longer they waited, the more time insurgents had to notice them and mount an attack.

The XO agreed. But even though Campbell repeatedly called and pleaded with him to come out after five minutes, it took the XO nearly another ten minutes to emerge—despite repeated promises that he was on his way. When the XO finally walked out, he was followed by twenty or so schoolkids. Just then, grenades started landing and, in Campbell's words, "the crowd of small children disintegrated into flame and smoke." In the ensuing firefight and efforts to get the kids to a hospital, Lance Corporal Todd Bolding had his legs blown off and later died. The men of Joker One were shaken by Bolding's loss, and Campbell became withdrawn and depressed for weeks. But his men remained loyal to him throughout and continued to step between him and enemy gunfire because they knew that although he couldn't protect them from everything, Campbell always had their backs.

The steps most bosses take to protect their people are less dramatic and risky. Yet a hallmark of effective bosses everywhere is that they doggedly protect their people. As we see in chapter 6, great bosses battle on their people's behalf—even when they suffer personally as a result.

THE MINDSET OF A GREAT BOSS

How Would Your People Answer These Questions About You?

1. **Following Lasorda's Law?** Are you constantly thinking about and trying to walk the most constructive line between being too assertive and not assertive enough? Or are you neglecting to give people the guidance, wisdom, and feedback they need to succeed? Worse yet, are you obsessively monitoring and micromanaging every move they make?

2. **Got Grit?** Do you treat the work you lead as a marathon or a sprint—are you dogged and patient, pressing yourself and your people ever forward? Or do you look for instant cures, treat life as one emergency after another, and give up (or disappear) when the going gets tough?

3. **Small Wins?** Do you frame what your people need to accomplish as a series of small, realistic, and not overly difficult steps? Or do you usually propose grand goals and strategies without helping people break them into bite-sized pieces?

4. **Beware the Toxic Tandem?** Do you remind yourself
   that your people are watching you very closely—and
   do you act accordingly to avoid doing little things that
   undermine their performance and dignity? Or are you
   oblivious to this intense scrutiny and rarely (if ever)
   think about how the little things you do and say will be
   magnified in your followers' minds?

5. **Got Their Backs?** Do you see your job as caring for
   and protecting your people, and fighting for them
   when necessary? Or do you consider it too much
   trouble to advocate for resources they need or too
   personally risky to battle idiocy from on high? When
   your people screw up, do you take the heat or hang
   them out to dry? When you screw up, do you admit it
   or point the finger of blame at your innocent
   underlings?

Performance and Humanity

Even though the journey is never easy, great bosses know
what goals to strive for and how the ride ought to feel
along the way—and lousy bosses never seem to quite get
it. A nasty law firm I once worked with demonstrates why
a boss's goals matter so much. The average partner in this
firm made close to a million dollars a year, but the firm
lost its soul in the process of bringing in all that wealth.
Nearly every partner I spoke with was hostile and rude; I
soon noticed they treated each other with similar disrespect. Many complained that it had become an oppressive
and mean-spirited place. Several partners were especially

upset because the firm's chair (let's call him Henry) had demeaned, exhausted, and driven out many skilled and admired attorneys in his quest to pump up billed hours and profits per partner. As one weary older partner told me, "We used to pride ourselves for having the best balance of humanity and economics in the business. Under Henry's leadership, it is all economics all the time, humanity be damned."

This leads to my first lesson about goals: Bosses ought to be judged by what they and their people get done *and* by how their followers feel along the way. This is why Henry does not qualify as a great boss in my book. The best bosses balance performance and humanity, getting things done in ways that enhance rather than destroy dignity and pride. I am singing a tune much like psychologists Mark Van Vugt, Robert Hogan, and Robert Kaiser, who after examining research on tribes of hunter-gatherers and modern groups concluded that effective leaders are "both competent and benevolent." In my opinion, bosses who drive their people to make piles of money and crank out lots of work—but crush the human spirit along the way—are bad bosses.

The second lesson is that if someone claims they have a precise one-size-fits-all measure of "boss effectiveness" that can be applied anywhere, they are wrong. The metrics used by law firms, such as profits per partner and billable hours, may make sense for them but not for basketball coaches, Methodist ministers, 7-Eleven store managers, SWAT team captains, or the CEO of Wal-Mart. The best anyone can do is to identify general goals that great bosses aim for—like "performance" and "humanity." Then the specific metrics that reflect these broad aims must be developed for each setting.

The third lesson is that bosses, like other humans, are notoriously poor judges of their own actions and accomplishments. My conversations with Henry suggested that he was oblivious to the lack of humanity in his firm and in his abrasive style—even though his nastiness was widely known by firm insiders and industry outsiders. If you are boss, what do you think your people (and others) would say about you? It turns out that followers, peers, superiors, and customers consistently provide better information about a boss's strengths, weaknesses, and quirks than the boss him- or herself. Most people suffer from "self-enhancement bias" and believe they are better than the rest—and they have a hard time accepting or remembering contrary facts. One study showed, for example, that 90 percent of drivers believe they have above-average driving skills.

More to the point, the College Board's survey of nearly 1 million U.S. high school seniors found that 70 percent reported they had above-average leadership skills; only 2 percent reported having below-average skills.

This self-deception plagues experienced bosses, too: A study of naval officers showed that peer ratings predicted which officers would receive early promotions—self-evaluations did not. This pervasive self-enhancement bias helps explain why you probably know a few—or perhaps many—bosses who suffer from false and inflated views of themselves. I have met perhaps a dozen bosses over the years who claimed to be "level 5 leaders," selfless and relentless leaders who (as Jim Collins asserts in *Good to Great*) head the greatest companies. Yet, in every case where I had solid inside information, followers viewed these same bosses as selfish and incapable of putting their organization's needs ahead of their own. Beware if you fancy yourself as the rare boss who sees yourself as others do: Chances are you're deluding yourself. Most people believe that they make more accurate self-assessments than peers. Unfortunately, such confidence is often just another form of self-aggrandizement. Despite our beliefs to the contrary, most of us suffer the same distorted self-assessments as our colleagues. Worse yet, the most deeply incompetent people suffer from the most inflated assessments of their own abilities and performance.

The upshot is that great bosses work relentlessly toward two general kinds of goals—but whether or not they persistently achieve them is best judged by others:

1. **Performance.** Does the boss do everything possible to help people do great work? The ultimate judgment about the quality and quantity of the work is best made by outsiders rather than insiders. To borrow a theme from J. Richard Hackman's lifetime of research on team performance, great bosses and their followers produce work that consistently meets or exceeds the expectations of those who use and evaluate it.

Regardless of local jargon and metrics, as Robert Townsend insisted in *Up the Organization*, a boss's job is "to eliminate people's excuses for failure."

2. **Humanity.** Does the boss do everything possible to help people experience dignity and pride? A boss's humanity is usually best judged by insiders, especially followers. After scouring through over one hundred ethnographies of employees' work lives, Randy Hodson concluded that working with dignity means "taking actions that are worthy of respect by oneself and others." Dignity enables people to travel through their days feeling upbeat and respected.

There are times when a boss can spark both performance and humanity. In 2008, I spoke at a workshop for the Vermont Oxford Network, which links together hospitals to reduce medical errors and deaths in neonatal intensive care units (NICUs). There were several hundred NICU doctors, nurses, administrators, and parents in the room. Another speaker provided a stirring example of how the best doctors treat their colleagues (especially nurses) with greater humanity and, in doing so, provide better care to babies. Dr. Michael Giuliano asserted that when physicians ask nurses questions like "Do you agree with my diagnosis?" or "Please tell me anything you see that contradicts my diagnosis," nurses feel more respected—and physicians make more accurate diagnoses.

Unfortunately, such simultaneous two-for-one victories aren't always possible. Yet bosses can still sustain high levels of both performance and humanity if they remember that "time was invented so that you don't have to do everything at once." This notion is conveyed simply by David Kelley, chairman and founder of IDEO, one of the most renowned innovation firms in the world. When David talks about it, he draws a "love" and "money" sketch, which he was kind enough to reproduce for this book:

David sees his job, or the job of any boss, as enabling people to experience dignity and joy as they travel through their workdays (the love part, what I call humanity) *and* to do work that keeps the lights on and provides them with fair pay, health care, and other necessities (the money part, what I call performance). David says that although sometimes you can accomplish both at once, there are always stretches when people must do things they don't love to bring in money. David explains that great bosses work to strike a balance between love and money over time, for example, by making sure that a designer who has worked on a dull, frustrating, and lucrative project gets to choose an inspiring if less profitable project the next time.

Managers at IDEO don't accomplish this balancing act just through bigger moves like project assignments. They do it in little ways, too: When designers have been working like dogs and are tired, grumpy, and starting to bicker, managers find little ways to slow things down, have some fun, and promote civility and mutual respect. This might happen by making sure that a designer who has been grinding away designing a medical device can get a refreshing break by going to a brainstorming session, say, on how to improve the airport security experience, get doctors to wash their hands more frequently, or design new playing pieces for the Monopoly board game. Managers at IDEO also provide breaks by shooting darts from Nerf guns or launching rubber darts called Finger Blasters at their people—which often degenerate into full-scale fifteen-minute battles. Such adolescent antics won't work in every workplace. But when the performance pressure starts heating up and things are on the verge of turning ugly, skilled bosses everywhere find ways to give people a break, or tell a joke, or just make a warm gesture to place more weight on the "humanity" side of the scale. As David put it, "foam darts aren't for everybody, but there is always some form of play in every culture that allows people to let off steam."

The Zen of the Best Bosses

Performance and humanity are the goals that great bosses aim to achieve. Yet the best bosses devote little energy to thinking about how great it would be to reach these goals, worrying if they can, or even celebrating when they do. *Zen in the Art of Archery* shows why it is a mistake to think about your goals too much. Author Eugen Herrigel was a philosopher who visited Japan in the 1950s to learn archery from a Zen master. Herrigel learned to devote little attention to hitting the target. The Zen master taught him to focus on the pleasures and tiny nuances of breathing properly, attaching the string, setting the arrow in the bow, drawing it back, and releasing it, rather than on hitting the target itself. By focusing on these actions, Herrigel and fellow archery students were rewarded in two ways: they took more pleasure from doing each task, and since they learned to master the nuances (much like the small-wins strategy), they hit the target more consistently as well.

In the same spirit, if you want to be a great boss, devote your attention to the small steps that you and your people ought to take along the way. Doing so will help you enjoy your job more and pump up your odds of success. The next seven chapters dig into the nuances of these steps.

SECTION II

What the Best Bosses Do

CHAPTER 2

Take Control

If you want to be a successful boss, you have to convince people that your words and deeds pack a punch. If they don't believe you are in charge, your job will be impossible to do and your life will be hell. This chapter is about what it takes to magnify the illusion and reality that you are in control of what your followers do, how well they perform, and how they feel along the way.

As we've seen, bosses matter, especially to their immediate followers and in small teams and organizations. Yet they are not all powerful. Even though most of us realize that leaders have limited powers, we can't resist treating their words and deeds as the main drivers of performance. Research by James Meindl on "the romance of leadership" shows that leaders get far more credit and blame than they deserve from followers, bosses, and outsiders. Meindl found that most journalists, management experts, consultants, and employees attribute superhuman powers to the top dog regardless of the facts. This ingrained "cognitive error" happens because it is less taxing and more emotionally satisfying to treat leadership as the primary cause of performance than sorting through a convoluted hodgepodge of factors. Stories about leaders are vivid and intriguing; slogging through the multiple and often dull factors that actually cause performance is far less interesting. So it is less work and more fun to give bosses the lion's share of glory and guilt. This bias is especially strong in cultures that glorify heroes and rugged individuals, such as the United States, Canada, Australia, Israel, and most European countries.

Even though most of us know better, we are drawn to stories and studies that portray leaders as either superheroes or incompetent dolts. We love hearing about the seemingly magical powers of leaders like Apple's temperamental genius Steve Jobs, Procter & Gamble's modest and likeable former CEO A. G. Lafley, Pepsi's ambitious and determined CEO Indra K. Nooyi, wise billionaire investor Warren Buffett, star and business mogul Oprah Winfrey, and legendary UCLA basketball coach John Wooden. It is even harder to resist demonizing the bosses of failing organizations. I am, for example, still completely pissed off at the idiotic and overpaid former leaders of financial service firms including Lehman Brothers' Richard Fuld, AIG's Hank Greenberg, Bear Stearns's James Cayne, Merrill Lynch's John Thain, and Countrywide Financial's Angelo Mozilo for driving their companies—and the global economy—into the ground a couple years back. I despise these assholes for losing my money and everyone else's, even though as an organizational theorist, I know that blaming them for this entire mess is irrational.

The truth is that bosses of everything from small groups to Fortune 500 firms don't matter as much as most of us believe. They typically account for less than 15 percent of the gap between good and bad organizational performance, although they often get over 50 percent of the blame and credit. Bosses of small (and young) workplaces have the biggest impact, especially on human reactions like turnover, satisfaction, and health. Yet even those bosses are over-romanticized, and their impact is magnified in our minds. In fact, even when bosses have no influence at all, we still heap on the credit and blame. When experiments at Stanford and Caltech were rigged so it was impossible for leaders to influence team performance, members still gave the appointed "leader" most of the credit and blame. Members of poorly performing teams were even willing to spend their own money to get rid of their "lousy" (if irrelevant) leaders.

If you are a boss, this is your lot in life. You can't change it, so you better learn to deal with it.

Fueling the Illusion and Reality of Control

The best bosses recognize they can't reverse the romance of leadership, but they can use it to their advantage. They take steps to magnify the illusion that they are in control.

As Max DePree, former CEO of furniture maker Herman Miller, put it, "The first job of a leader is to define reality." Talented bosses aren't, however, just con men (and women) who use psychological smoke and mirrors to create the illusion they are in charge. The strange twist is that by enhancing the *illusion* they are in control, bosses increase their *actual* control over what their followers do, how they feel along the way, and how glowingly their work is evaluated by outsiders.

Act Like You Are in Control, Even When You Aren't

Andy Grove was tremendously successful as Intel's CEO. Growth and earnings went through the roof during his tenure. He was selected *Time* magazine's Man of the Year in 1997. Grove is one of the most blunt executives I've ever met. In 2002, I was at a conference in Silicon Valley where Andy was interviewed by Harvard's Clay Christensen. Clay asked Andy how leaders could act and feel confident despite their doubts. Andy began by talking about the *Sopranos* TV show and how intrigued he was by fictional mob boss Tony Soprano's struggles. The messes that Tony dealt with week after week included turf wars, unexpected hits on Tony's people, bad decisions, emotionally unstable subordinates, and Uncle Junior, who kept undermining his authority and trust. Andy commented that although Soprano's product was different from Intel's, "anybody in this room could very easily relate" to his daily struggles to maintain control.

After the laughter died down, Andy said, "Investment decisions or personnel decisions and prioritization don't wait for that picture to be clarified. You have to make them when you have to make them. So you take your shots and clean up the bad ones later." He added, "So you have to keep your own spirits up *even though you well understand that you don't know what you're doing.*" The emphasis is mine: Grove's honesty was stunning. A minute or so later, Andy explained what I would call faking it until you make it: "Well, part of it is self-discipline and part of it is deception. And the deception becomes reality. It is deception in the sense that you pump yourself up and put a better face on things than you start off feeling. But after a while, if you act confident, you become more confident. So the deception becomes less of a deception."

Grove's advice echoes evidence on effective leaders, from case studies of great generals to experiments with MBAs. His argument that acting confident makes you feel confident is supported by research on attitude change, which shows "belief follows behavior": Acting confident will help you become confident. Confidence is also important because, like all emotions, it is contagious and will spread to followers.

This is one reason that General George Washington was effective, even though he screwed up constantly when learning the job. Washington made many mistakes, like putting his faith in lousy subordinates, making bad decisions that killed many soldiers, and suffering from bouts of indecision. But he always looked and acted confidently in charge. As historian David McCullough tells us in *1776*, Washington was impeccably clean, a first-rate horseman, and carried himself "like a soldier" who had "the look and bearing of a man accustomed to respect and being obeyed." "Faking it until you make it" can trigger a self-fulfilling prophecy: by acting as if you know what you are doing and are in control, even if it isn't true at first, such confidence can inspire you and others to achieve great performance—as Andy Grove and George Washington demonstrated.

The ability to convey confidence isn't something most bosses are born with; they learn it through mentoring and experience. Consider Goldman Sachs CEO Lloyd Blankfein, who led the giant investment bank through the ups and downs of the financial meltdown. Blankfein has been credited for his steadiness and confidence throughout the brutal crisis and for helping Goldman emerge from it in far better shape than most competitors (albeit via some mighty controversial moves). He wasn't always so confident. Blankfein described how, on the first day he took charge of the foreign exchange business, it immediately started losing money. He became very nervous and went to his boss to propose a plan for reversing the losses. Blankfein's boss told him it sounded good and he should implement it—then added some valuable advice:

> I turned to walk out of the room, and he said: "Lloyd, just one second before you go. Why don't you stop in the men's room first and throw some water on

your face, because if people see you looking as green as you look, they'll jump out the window." ... I learned in general about how important that kind of symbolism is and how you can inspire or defeat confidence.

Bosses do many small things to create confidence that they are in charge and then spread it to others: See "Tricks for Taking Charge" at the end of the chapter. These small wins range from interrupting people to flashing a bit of anger, crossing your arms, or giving away a bit of power.

Confidence is contagious and increases your odds of success, but it isn't a magic bullet. You need other things to succeed—resources, a viable technology, a market for your product or services, and so on. Consider Bill Campbell's experience at GO Corporation. Bill is one of the most respected bosses and mentors in Silicon Valley. He is affectionately known as "the coach" because he was the head coach of Columbia University's football team. Bill has played central roles in growing many companies, including as founding CEO of Claris, and now serves as Intuit's chairman and as an Apple board member. Bill has mentored dozens of successful bosses, from Google's executive team to Netscape cofounder Marc Andreesen. Bill also is among Steve Jobs's most trusted advisors. Yet even Bill's confidence and ability couldn't save GO, a pen-based computing company he ran in the early 1990s. GO had backing from renowned venture capitalist John Doerr, and Bill was surrounded with people who had grit and confidence in his abilities. Not a single member of his team left Bill during the time he was CEO, even though GO was in a downward spiral and closed in 1994. The technology remained promising, but the market for their product never materialized.

Why did people put their careers on the line when the writing was on the wall? Randy Komisar, a member of GO's senior team, reports that Bill never stopped trying to find ways to succeed, and everyone understood his commitment to them and the company. Bill was always open, realistic about the risk, but confident about the potential. He communicated with every employee about their collective challenges at company meetings, staff meetings, and one-on-ones. They felt empowered, not hoodwinked. To the bitter end, Bill was on airplanes to Asia and Europe trying to find a way forward. His people trusted Bill to be there when they needed him, even in the company's death throes. Bill and John Doerr sold the company to AT&T without any return to investors in order to save as many jobs as possible—and spent months finding jobs for displaced employees.

Great bosses use confidence and other means to enhance control. But there are no surefire paths to success, and anyone who tries to sell you magical cures is a liar.

Don't Dither—Say Yes or No

Indecision is a hallmark of crummy bosses. In *The Peter Principle*, Laurence Peter and Raymond Hull dubbed this the Teeter-Totter Syndrome: "An employee of this type can balance endlessly and minutely the pros and cons of a question but cannot come down on one side of the question or the other....He usually deals with the problems that come to him by keeping them in limbo until someone else makes the decision or until it is too late for a solution."

The best bosses, in contrast, realize that making crisp decisions bolsters their control. Definitive decisions make it easier for people to know what to do next. Answering employees with a clear yes or no, and doing so quickly, is especially constructive. If the answer to a suggestion or request is yes, then people can move to implement it. If the answer is an unambiguous no, they can turn their labors elsewhere. I love the advice given about saying yes and no by the late Frank Hauser, whom I introduced in chapter 1. Hauser directed many award-winning plays and was adored by actors. He advised:

> Please, PLEASE be decisive.
> As the director, you have three weapons: "Yes," "No," and "I don't know." Use them. Don't dither; you can always change your mind later. Nobody minds that. What they do mind is the two-minute agonizing when all the actor has asked is, "Do I get up now?"

Of course, the dithering can go on a lot longer than two minutes for bosses who suffer from the Teeter-Totter Syndrome. Academic administrators are especially infamous for this disease, as many lack the courage to tell faculty (many of whom are temperamental assholes) a firm no, so they stall, say, "Maybe, I have to think about it," and never get around to giving a firm answer. I've learned to prefer the rare administrators who say no rather than maybe. I recently received a firm no from Academic Director Bernie Roth for my request to teach an innovation class in the Hasso Plattner Institute of Design, also known as "the Stanford d.school." For a few seconds, I was indignant because, after all, I am a cofounder of the d.school, and I believed the class fit our mission. Then it struck me: Bernie had said no right away and did so clearly—a rare treat in academia. So I wrote Bernie an e-mail praising him profusely for his clear decision and encouraged him to keep it up, with me and others.

Get and Give Credit

A wonderful thing about being the boss is that when your people do good work, you usually get more credit than you deserve. Smart bosses help this process along. Sure, some grab excessive credit because they are arrogant blowhards. But effective bosses also do it because, to be seen as competent, the people they are beholden to need to believe there is a strong link between their actions and performance. People want to oversee, work for, and patronize winners, and it comforts and calms them to believe the boss is in control.

The gyrations required to get credit for good things and to make such accomplishments seem even more wonderful are standard fare in organizational life, especially for bosses. Most learn how to brag without coming across as braggarts during job interviews, performance evaluations, and interactions with customers and clients in order to survive and thrive in their careers. If you are a boss, you probably already know and use subtle tactics such as collaborating with others who will praise your efforts so you don't have to come across as a glory hog, bragging about your coworkers in turn, pointing to your (seemingly) objective accomplishments, and giving copious credit to others when talking about your successes.

This last tactic is especially crucial for being seen as a boss who is both in charge and humane. In fact, I recommend giving your followers *more credit* than you believe they deserve. Let me explain. For starters, the people who usually give a boss the *least* credit are their immediate followers. After all, they usually know the facts about who did what better than outsiders. I remember hanging out at IDEO some years back and talking with some designers about a magazine that had published a huge picture of then CEO (and now chairman) David Kelley and a claim he designed over three thousand products. Nearly all of those products were designed by David's employees, not him. David was busy running the company and landing clients. This is the romance of leadership in action and it is tough to stop—especially with the press; they love stories that feature heroic and all-powerful leaders, because that kind of stuff sells.

No matter how much credit you give your people, the

romance of leadership means you—as the boss—will probably get more than you deserve from outsiders. A host of studies on "overclaiming" muddies things further. Individuals consistently give themselves more credit for their team's productivity than they deserve: When people in four- or five-person teams are each asked privately to estimate what percentage they contributed to the group's product, the total usually adds up to around 150 percent. This research means that you, dear boss, are also prone to privately (and perhaps publically) giving yourself more credit than you deserve.

Everyone wins if you can bring yourself to give your people as much credit as possible and take as little as possible. You get tons of credit anyway because you are the boss; your people will see you as more truthful, and you will be admired (especially by outsiders) for your modesty and generosity.

Now, let's return to IDEO's David Kelley, who is unusually generous about giving others credit. David is modest and cares a great deal for his people. His intentions are pure, but his generosity still helps him and other managers at IDEO convince people that they are in control on both the performance and humanity fronts. As we saw in chapter 1, David sees a big part of his job as striking a healthy balance between these two sometimes conflicting goals. In 2000, *BusinessWeek* approached IDEO to generate ideas for a big spread on products of the future, called "Welcome to 2010." A team of designers worked like dogs to develop images of a dozen or so products they imagined might be available by 2010. Some of these ideas were nearly on target, such as the tiny phone that fits in your ear and the E-map, which seemed a lot like a small, thin global positioning system. Other ideas still seem a little further away even now, like the home medical mirror, which enables your doctor to examine you over the Internet rather than in the office.

When this flashy eight-page spread was almost done, *BusinessWeek*'s editors called David and told him there was no room to print the names of the IDEO designers. David politely fought back, arguing they worked like crazy on it, he had promised them credit, and it wasn't fair to give him all the credit. The editors backed off and listed Martin Bone, Tom Eich, Thomas Enders, Rick English, and Danny Stilton as the creative team. These designers were grateful for how hard David fought for them; the *BusinessWeek* editors were impressed by David's generosity—and he still got plenty of credit for a great piece. I talked to David about this episode recently, when he drew the sketch shown in chapter 1 about the skill and self-awareness bosses need to balance humanity and performance over time. David argued that bosses should never pass up the chance to "build up love points with their people" because "the time will come when you will need to do something on the economics side that will burn up those points." In other words, giving people the credit they deserve, and more, helps bosses exercise more perceived and objective control over events—and strike a balance between performance and humanity over the long haul, too.

Blame Yourself

In late August 2008, I was listening to public radio, and on came CEO Michael McCain of Maple Leaf Foods. McCain made a statement and took press questions about the (ultimately) twenty deaths and hundreds of illnesses traced to Listeria (a form of bacteria) in meats produced in his Maple Leaf plant. McCain sounded somber and his voice quivered as he announced the plant was closed, apologized to those hurt by his firm's products, and admitted that people at Maple Leaf—including himself—were responsible for the tragedy. In answering questions, McCain refused to blame government inspectors for the deaths and stated that he and his people simply had not done their jobs well enough. He then went into detail about the steps that Maple Leaf was already planning (e.g., more rigorous inspection) and emphasized that it was his job to restore the faith of the Canadian people in Maple Leaf.

McCain's response was striking, both because it is so rare and because it is so consistent with research on how to fuel the illusion (and reality) that a boss is in charge. Unlike most bosses in this situation, McCain accepted that he would get blamed no matter what he did. Rather than ducking and dodging and pointing fingers at others, he realized it was wiser to accept it, learn from it, and do what he could to make the best of the horrible situation. In addition to being seen as disingenuous, leaders who blame forces outside the organization exclusively for their troubles create the impression of powerlessness. By refusing to take any responsibility, bosses raise an implicit and damning question: "If you didn't have the power to break it, how can we expect you to have the power to fix it?" Refusal to accept responsibility is also seen as a sign that nothing was learned—or will be changed—as a result of past setbacks and errors.

Another misguided trick that bosses use when things go wrong is to use mealymouthed language like "mistakes were made," a phrase the late William Safire defined in his *Political Dictionary* as "[a] passive-evasive way of acknowledging error while distancing the speaker from responsibility for it" and other commentators describe as a classic non-apology apology. For example, Chairman of the Board J. R. Crespo admitted that "Clearly, mistakes were made" and called them "embarrassing" when reporters discovered that managers at the Yale–New Haven Hospital had been instructed to fight a union-organizing drive by presenting arguments that (in my opinion) were mean-spirited and intended to arouse fear and suspicion of the union. During a "Response Team Employee Relations Workshop," managers were given a handout titled "Conduct During Organizing Campaign—Things You *May* Do." These tips included:

Tell employees about documented history of Mafia influence and corruption of unions. Tell employees examples of where union leaders have embezzled money from their members' pension and health insurance funds.

Crespo wrote a letter to New Haven's mayor John DeStefano that admitted these and other mistakes had happened and were violations of a written agreement between the union and the hospital. But Crespo and his board appeared to accept no responsibility for these mistakes, offered no apology, did not admit to any harm or suffering caused by these instructions (except their own embarrassment), and emphasized that senior management was not aware of this or other admittedly inaccurate information (e.g., employees would lose pay and benefits if they voted for the union). Crespo also indicated that they had fired the consultants and HR people involved in the fiasco—implicitly deflecting blame.

Refusal to accept blame, pointing fingers at others, and wimpy language can help bosses keep their jobs for a while, but it usually backfires in the long run. No matter what is said, bosses are seen as responsible for what their people do. When something important happens (such as training that links unions to the Mafia), the boss is expected to know. If you as a boss want to enhance the illusion and reality of control, and fuel performance, too, taking at least some of the blame is usually a better path. Experiments by Fiona Lee and her colleagues show that managers who took responsibility for bad events like pay freezes and failed projects were seen as more powerful, competent, and likable than those who denied responsibility. Lee and her colleagues did another study, titled "Mea Culpa," which examined stock price changes in fourteen companies over a twenty-one-year stretch. They found that when senior management blamed their firms' recent troubles on internal and controllable factors (and took blame themselves) stock prices were consistently higher the next year, compared to when executives denied responsibility for setbacks. An earlier study that tracked the performance of eighteen firms over eighteen years produced similar results.

The key here is not just to accept blame and apologize. Bosses need to take immediate control over whatever they can, show they have learned from failures, announce new plans, and—when changes are implemented—make sure that everyone knows they have wrestled back control over the situation. The list below, "A Recipe for an Effective Apology," outlines seven ingredients for taking blame effectively and illustrates each with actions by McCain and his team. No one can predict the ultimate fate of Maple Leaf Foods; only time will tell if they can avoid another Listeria outbreak and sustain consumer confidence over the long run. But McCain's actions during the early months of the crisis demonstrate a recipe for the right way to take blame. The Canadian press and public relations experts gave McCain high marks for clarity, compassion, and control. A company spokesperson also announced a poll in early December 2008 indicating that confidence in the Maple Leaf brand had risen from 60 percent to 91 percent since the crisis began. Maple Leaf suffered a far more dramatic setback than most bosses have to deal with, but the steps taken—in concert with McCain's steadiness and humanity—demonstrate how great bosses convince others they are in control when the shit hits the fan.

As Barbara Kellerman shows in the *Harvard Business Review*, "Even when an apology is too late, it does not need to be too little." Kellerman describes how Duke Hospital made the mistake of transplanting the wrong heart and lungs into a teenage girl, who died as a result. Although Duke CEO Ralph Snyderman was silent at first, he responded to an onslaught of media criticism with remorse, openness, and honesty: "No fewer than nine press releases were issued in five days, and Snyderman agreed to be interviewed by Ed Bradley on *60 Minutes*. On camera, Snyderman admitted the mistake, took responsibility, expressed remorse, and vowed that the hospital would do everything it could to preclude such a calamity from ever happening again."

A RECIPE FOR AN EFFECTIVE APOLOGY
Michael McCain at Maple Leaf Foods

REMEMBER—The key here was that CEO McCain took the blame himself. He didn't put it on his employees, outsiders, or events he could not control!

No sugar coating. McCain emphasized how horrible the deaths and illnesses from the Listeria in his plant were, without a hint of waffling.

Take the blame fully. "Our best efforts failed." McCain refused to blame government inspectors for the deaths.

Apologize fully. "We are deeply sorry."

Take immediate control over what you can. The plant was shut, products were recalled, extreme efforts were made to pull products from stores, and an aggressive media campaign was launched to warn consumers to discard contaminated meats.

Explain what you have learned. McCain went on national TV and YouTube to describe how, after working with authorities for weeks, they discovered multiple places in the plant where their usual "deep cleaning" procedures had failed to reach.

Communicate what you will do differently. McCain announced plans to implement deep cleaning and many other procedures, put the Maple Leaf Foods Action Plan on the company website, and used near-daily press conferences, plus television and newspaper ads, to describe steps his team was taking and their commitment to putting customers' health first.

Get credit for improvements. McCain announced in a TV advertisement and YouTube video, "I promised you that Maple Leaf will always put food safety first and we have. The recall is over and the problems that led to it have been fixed." He announced the implementation of over two hundred procedures, including daily sanitization of slicing equipment; biweekly deep cleansing of each line, and a massive increase in testing the meats.

Bosses who oversee small teams and organizations have an especially tough time arguing that they aren't to blame for screwups. Think of the doctor who led that failed surgical team at Duke, an owner-operator of an auto shop that botches your car repair, or the manager of a baseball team. Because such leaders interact so directly and personally with their charges, and may do some of the work themselves, their impact on performance seems especially strong to both insiders and outsiders. The best become remarkably adept at taking blame when things go badly, demonstrating what they have learned and are doing differently as a result—and saying and doing things to reinforce the message that they deserve much credit when performance is good. Joe Torre managed the New York Yankees baseball team for twelve years amid constant criticism and second-guessing from the hypercritical New York media and fans, as well as from George Steinbrenner, the temperamental, overbearing, and impatient Yankees owner. One reason that Torre endured in one of the most difficult jobs in sports (before he arrived, Steinbrenner had fired seventeen managers in eighteen years) was because he routinely accepted blame and admitted mistakes after losses and other mishaps—both in media interviews and private conversations with the volatile Steinbrenner. Torre emphasized what his team was learning from the setbacks, what he thought they could change, and also what he believed they couldn't control. Taking the heat, talking about what they would do differently, and expressing confidence that things would improve helped protect Torre's players from attacks by the media and Steinbrenner; also, when the Yankees did win games and championships (and they won a lot), Torre was seen as in control of his team's performance.

Torre left the Yankees in 2007 and now manages the

Los Angeles Dodgers, where he continues to play the blame (and credit) game masterfully. Reporters asked him in early June 2009 whether he expected the first-place Dodgers to hold their lead, even though star player Manny Ramirez had been suspended until July for using steroids. Torre replied that the team was playing plenty well, so "if anything goes bad I screwed up, no question." Torre's willingness to accept blame for future setbacks shows how, to get and keep a management job, skilled bosses talk and act as if there is a strong link between their actions and followers' performance. Torre also displays the subtle art of taking credit for performance without bragging: He left unsaid, yet still made clear, that he deserved credit for all those games that the Dodgers were winning without their star. Indeed, the Dodgers still held a commanding lead in their division when Ramirez returned on July 3.

Powers and Limits

Effective bosses are confident in their ability to influence the events that swirl around them, and skilled at enticing others to believe in and act on such powers. The worst bosses, the powerless ones, are punished with unfaithful followers, irate customers, and ugly moments with their superiors. But even the best bosses are bedeviled with shortcomings. No matter how much credit or blame they get, bosses have limited control. Every boss acts on incomplete information. Every boss suffers from bouts of overconfidence and insecurity.

Every boss is cursed with weaknesses and blind spots that can be overcome only with help from others. The best bosses and worst bosses are similar in that both have deep flaws. They are different, however, in that the best have the wisdom and self-awareness to stem the damage caused by their frailties, as the next chapter shows.

TRICKS FOR TAKING CHARGE

WARNING!! Learn to be just assertive enough! Don't become an overbearing asshole when you use these strategies!

1. **Talk more than others—but not the whole time.** This is sometimes called "the babble" or "blabbermouth" theory of leadership. At least in Western countries, people who talk first and most are usually seen as "our leaders" and "most influential." But don't talk the whole time, as people will see you as a bully, boring, or both.

2. **Interrupt people occasionally—and don't let them interrupt you much.** People gain power by winning "interruption wars," interjecting and battling back when others try to interrupt.

3. **Cross your arms when you talk.** When people cross their arms, they persist longer and generate more solutions when working on difficult tasks. Crossing your arms sends yourself a message to crank up the grit and confidence—but beware that doing it too much and too intensely can make you look like an uptight jerk.

4. **Use positive self-talk.** This isn't just a fuzzy new-age idea. People who make encouraging statements to themselves enjoy higher self-esteem and performance. The most effective self-talk focuses on encouraging yourself ("You've done this before") and applying specific strategies ("Lean hard, now").

5. **Try a little flash of anger now and then.** As studies by Stanford professor Larissa Tiedens show, using anger strategically via outbursts, snarling looks, and hand gestures like pointing and jabbing "create the impression that the expresser is competent." So, used in small doses and with proper precautions, flashes of anger can help you seize control. But spewing out constant venom undermines your authority and will earn you a well-deserved reputation as an asshole.

6. **If you are not sure whether to sit down or stand up, stand up.** This is especially crucial if you are a new boss. Standing up signals you are in charge and encourages others to accept your authority. Also, whether you sit or stand, sit at the head of the table (at least in Western countries).

7. **Ask your people what they need to succeed and then try to give it to them.** Obvious, isn't it? It is also remarkably rare.

8. **Tell people about your pet peeves and quirks.** It isn't just the big things that can make or break perceptions that you are a good boss. Psychologist Ben Dattner suggests writing a "Managerial User's Manual" for your team if you are a new boss, where "you can describe your preferences, your style, what makes you apoplectic, and what people may not understand about you."

9. **Give away some power or status, but make sure everyone knows it was your choice.** One of the most effective ways to show that you are powerful and benevolent is to accept—even bargain for—some status symbol for yourself and then to give it to others. One CEO I work with started out in a huge corner office. But as he established authority in other ways and realized there was a space crunch, he moved to a much smaller office so his big one could be shared by four employees.

CHAPTER 3

Strive to Be Wise

The best bosses dance on the edge of overconfidence, but a healthy dose of self-doubt and humility saves them from turning arrogant and pigheaded. Bosses who fail to strike this balance are incompetent, dangerous to follow, and downright demeaning.

Consider a talkative senior executive who led a project team meeting I attended at a large corporation. I'll call her Roberta. She joked that a key to her success was that although she appeared to be listening to others, she usually wasn't. Rather, she used the time to "reload," to prepare what to say next. Roberta's joke described her behavior all too well. She spent much of the day spewing out short speeches that were irrelevant to the team's task or to what we had been talking about before she interjected (after all, she wasn't listening, she was "reloading"). At one juncture, an exasperated underling leaned over to me and whispered a list of the company's canned PowerPoint presentations that Roberta had been regurgitating at seemingly random intervals—and added, "As usual, Roberta is all transmission and no reception."

Roberta not only didn't listen, she asked few questions. This blabbering boss learned little from the smart people in the room, gave them no useful direction, and undermined their dignity, as none felt heard or respected. Roberta should have heeded Coach John Wooden's advice: "Listen to those under your supervision. Really listen. Don't act as if you're listening and let it go in one ear and out the other. Faking it is worse than not doing it at all."

As Roberta demonstrated, bad bosses sometimes come in bodies that can't listen. She was plenty smart, but lacked wisdom. Wisdom sounds like a fancy word, but the way I use it is pretty simple, thanks to psychologists John Meacham and Karl Weick. Wise bosses are devoted to knowing what they don't know. They act boldly on facts they have right now, but search for signs they are wrong—seeking a healthy balance between courage and humility. Roberta didn't suffer from excessive insecurity and self-doubt (as some unwise people do); she swerved toward arrogance.

The table that follows, "The Attitude of Wisdom," contrasts smart and wise bosses. There are plenty of times when bosses ought to act smart, when they need to make definitive statements, give intelligent answers, be skilled talkers, and defend a course of action. As we saw in chapter 2, bosses demonstrate they are in control through such means. Unfortunately, I never saw a hint that Roberta leavened her smarts with wisdom. She never expressed uncertainty, asked questions, really listened, asked for help, or challenged her own beliefs. Roberta's opinions were so strongly held that it was impossible to penetrate them with opposing opinions, logic, or facts. In contrast, to steal a phrase from futurist Paul Saffo, wise bosses have strong opinions that are weakly held—so they can update when confronted with contrary facts.

THE ATTITUDE OF WISDOM

Smart Versus Wise Bosses

Smart Bosses: Have the *confidence* to act on what they know, but feel and express *little doubt* (in public or private) about what they believe or do	**Wise Bosses:** Have the *confidence* to act on what they know and the *humility* to doubt their knowledge
Actions	**Actions**
Make definitive statements	Make statements (often "backstage") that reveal uncertainty and confusion
Answer questions	Ask questions
Talk well	Listen well
Give help, but don't ask for help and refuse it when offered	Give help, ask for help, and accept it when offered.
Defend and stick to current course of action—have strong opinions that are strongly held	Challenge and often revise courses of action—have strong opinions that are weakly held

Many of the skilled bosses in the last chapter coupled confidence with humility. Director Frank Hauser advocated decisiveness, but added "you can always change your mind later." George Washington's soldiers were swayed by his self-assurance, yet, as David McCullough reports in *1776*: "There was no hint of arrogance. 'Amiable' and 'modest' were the words most frequently used to describe him." Andy Grove urged confident action even when managers don't know what they are doing, but recommended: "Act on your temporary conviction as if it was a real conviction; and when you realize that you are wrong, correct course very quickly." Grove's advice captures the attitude of wisdom: being confident enough to act and humble enough to doubt your actions. This chapter digs into what it takes to develop and act on an attitude of wisdom

Safety, Failure, and Learning

Psychological safety is the key to creating a workplace where people can be confident enough to act without undue fear of being ridiculed, punished, or fired—and be humble enough to openly doubt what is believed and done. As Amy Edmondson's research shows, psychological safety emerges when those in power persistently praise, reward, and promote people who have the courage to act, talk about their doubts, successes, and failures, and work doggedly to do things better the next time. Edmondson learned the power of safety when studying drug treatment errors in hospital nursing units. To her amazement, the best nursing unit, where the boss encouraged nurses to talk openly about mistakes—and never pointed an angry finger of blame—reported about *ten times* more errors than the worst, fear-ridden unit. When nurses made or reported mistakes in the nasty unit, the leader treated them as "guilty" and "like a two-year-old." This tenfold difference in reported errors was due to psychological safety, not the actual error rate. Nurses with good bosses felt safe to admit mistakes; nurses with bad bosses avoided reporting errors because doing so provoked humiliation and retribution.

Promoting psychological safety also means that you, as boss, ought to admit your foibles to yourself and others. I described earlier how Dr. Michael Giuliano pressed doctors in neonatal intensive care units (NICUs) to invite others to question their diagnoses. Giuliano urges doctors to make the best diagnosis they can and act on it, but to keep searching for signs they are wrong. Giuliano provides concrete commandments including:

"Don't fall in love with your first diagnosis."

"Listen to the family." (Doctors are notoriously lousy listeners.)

"Don't believe everything you hear about the test results." (Check them yourself and make an independent judgment.)

"Explain everything to everyone." (The more people that understand what you are doing and why, the more help you can get.)

"Say 'I don't know' regularly and go get the answer."

Safety also means that you, as a boss, may end up encouraging people to do things that annoy you. Sticking to health care, Anita Tucker and Amy Edmondson identified nurses most likely to promote learning: noisy complainers and troublemakers who talked openly about their mistakes and those by colleagues. They were also "disruptive questioners," who kept asking why things were done that way and suggesting better ways. As Tucker and Edmondson say, most doctors define a good nurse as the exact opposite: one that is seen and not heard, who obediently follows orders, and refrains from questioning their actions.

The deadly double whammy of a lack of psychological safety and fear of authority are confirmed by some disconcerting research. A study in flight simulators by a major airline showed that when pilots faked mild incapacitation during the final stages of a landing in rough and rainy conditions, copilots failed to take the controls approximately 25 percent of the time—resulting in a simulated crash. The copilots all realized their pilots were incapacitated, yet still hesitated to question their authority. Unfortunately, dysfunctional deference causes real crashes, too. In 1979, the crash of a commuter plane apparently happened, in part, because the second officer (still on probation) failed to take control when the captain (a vice president known for his gruff style) became partly incapacitated. The settings differ, but the lesson is the same: when people don't feel safe—let alone obligated—to point out concerns, jump in, and correct their boss's mistakes, then learning and error correction grind to a halt.

Forgive and Remember

I saw the power of psychological safety at a large media company. The CEO was determined to drive fear out of his company. One executive had spent a year launching a new magazine. It flopped, which would have resulted in a demotion or a firing in past regimes. Instead, the CEO stood up at a gathering of the firm's top executives and congratulated the failed executive for her courage and skill, for doing the wrong thing in the right way. He emphasized that the ill-fated decision wasn't just hers; senior management backed it, and the magazine failed despite great content and marketing. In the following days, every executive I spoke with in the firm portrayed the CEO's actions as a watershed event, a visible step toward driving out fear.

This CEO's words and deeds demonstrate the best diagnostic question for assessing if a boss is creating or killing psychological safety: *What happens when people make mistakes or fail?* Jeff Pfeffer and I argue there are three kinds of reactions to failure. The first is to remember, blame, humiliate, and perhaps expel the culprit. This is the "do it right the first time or don't do it" mentality, which Amy Edmondson found in the unit where nurses were treated like two-year-olds. I have seen this fear-based approach in so many of the firms around Stanford University that I call it "the Silicon Valley standard." The second kind of reaction is "forgive and forget," which is what benevolent but incompetent bosses do. This is the approach that my teenagers hope for from their parents—such as the day my (then) sixteen-year-old daughter accidently stepped on the gas rather than the brake, crashed into our house, and did $1,000 in damage to a new car. She didn't want to talk about it; she wanted us to "forgive and forget." The third approach is what we try to use with our daughter, the one used by bosses who create safety and accountability: *forgive and remember.* This phrase is from research on how good hospitals learn from mistakes, and reflects both what the best leaders did in Edmondson's research and how that media CEO reacted to the failed magazine—they used failures as an opportunity for learning rather than finger pointing.

Psychological Safety and Creativity

The best bosses spark collective imagination by creating a safety zone where people can talk about twisted and half-baked ideas, test them, and fail without ridicule, punishment, or ostracism—and to fail cheaply and without doing harm to others. This is why IDEO's Diego Rodriguez (who also teaches at Stanford and writes the blog Metacool) asks bosses who want more creativity: "Where is your place for failing?" I adore this question because creativity requires generating many ideas—most of which are bad. It requires judging ideas honestly and openly and then discarding most. In the hands of a bad boss, this process embarrasses and stifles people who develop ideas that don't make the cut—and degrades the quality of those that are selected, developed, and thrown into the marketplace.

The writers of *The Onion* have a place to fail: meetings that last for days. *The Onion* is a newspaper and website that parodies the news, with stories like: "Cranberry Juice Industry Hoping 2009 A Big Year for Urinary Tract Infections," "Incompetent Staff Feels Underappreciated," and (really) "Study: Not Being an Asshole Boss May Boost Employee Morale." *The Onion* claims over 3 million print readers and 35 million monthly page views. Their process, led by Senior Editor Joe Randazzo, entails a grueling three-day brainstorming session each week. The team sits in a stuffy room and writers pitch one headline after another—those that the group finds funny (at least initially) are put on the board. About six hundred headlines are pitched the first day, which are ultimately culled to eighteen—and then turned into stories for the weekly paper.

Randazzo leads these sessions lightly because everyone understands they are expected to toss out crazy ideas and be critical—and over 95 percent of their ideas won't survive. Randazzo was described by the *Washington Post* as "an unassuming 30-year-old who doesn't radiate any bossish swagger in meetings and whom no one on the staff seems scared of or desperate to impress." He does intervene now and then to keep things safe and moving along: "There are times when a joke gets mired in semantics, and I have to tell everybody to shut the hell up. But that happens pretty rarely, probably once every couple of issues, when a story needs a definitive yes or no." Randazzo understands that if people feel inhibited about proposing extreme, dumb, or tasteless ideas, their collective creativity will grind to a halt.

Wisdom and Bad Assumptions

Wisdom helps bosses avoid falling prey to flawed assumptions. Wise bosses realize they are prone to what sociologist Ron Westrum calls "the fallacy of centrality": the misguided belief that because you are in a central position, if something important is going on, you will know about it. This fallacy kept pediatricians from diagnosing child abuse until the early 1960s: "Their reasoning? If parents were abusing children, I'd know about it; since I don't know about it, it isn't happening."

Most bosses are too busy (and too human) to know every important thing. Their ignorance is often amplified because, as research on the "mum effect" shows, followers hesitate to deliver bad news for fear the boss will "shoot the messenger." The mum effect may have contributed to the collapse of insurance giant AIG during the 2008 financial crisis—which survives only because of a mind-boggling 180-billion-dollar bailout from U.S. taxpayers. Michael Lewis wrote in *Vanity Fair* about how the culture in AIG's Financial Products unit changed for the worse after the touchy and temperamental Joe Cassano took charge in 2001—a job he held until 2008. Cassano's unit ultimately lost an estimated 45 billion dollars. AIG insiders told Lewis that the "debate and discussion that was common" under prior boss Tom Savage ground to a halt under Cassano. One explained, "The fear level was so high that...you presented what you did not to upset him. And if you were critical of the organization, all hell would break loose." Another added, "The way you dealt with Joe was to start everything by saying, 'You're right Joe.'" Lewis reported most executives with the courage to challenge Cassano quit out of frustration well before Financial Products start suffering those huge losses. Certainly, it isn't fair to blame all of AIG's troubles on Cassano, let alone the entire financial meltdown. Yet I agree with Lewis that Cassano's "crime was not mere legal fraudulence but the deeper kind: a need for subservience in others and an unwillingness to acknowledge his own weaknesses."

Cassano sounds like a certified asshole to me. But even the nicest bosses unwittingly reward followers who shield them from bad news. The executive assistant to one beloved CEO explained to me how, by controlling his schedule and calls, she controlled his moods. She adored her boss and hated to see him unhappy, and her job was no fun when he was grumpy. So she screened out appointment requests from people who put him in a foul mood, including those who usually delivered bad news or were known complainers.

Wise bosses don't just encourage followers to reveal bad news. They dig for evidence that clashes with their presumptions. Veteran project manager Paul Snare tells how, in a Pampers diaper plant in Michigan, supervisors believed their best mechanic wasn't documenting his work because he wanted to maintain an information edge over coworkers. They also believed he was strongly pro-union and resisted providing information that could help supervisors run the plant during a strike. These assumptions were dashed when a foreman asked the mechanic why he wasn't writing things down: "His answer was simple: He felt he had lousy penmanship and was ashamed to have his writing on display." Snare concludes, "Walk around, look, ask questions. Asking a question is the best source of information, yet it is the least used."

People are especially prone to making bad assumptions when they conclude things are completely routine and unfolding exactly as they expect. They go on automatic pilot, or "robot," and do what they always do without thinking about it much. Research on forest fires that burn out of control, surgical errors, and airplane crashes show that such horrible things can happen because rather than noticing signs that something is amiss, people keep mindlessly applying standard operating procedures without noticing ominous warning signs. To battle such blind spots, Karl Weick and Kathleen Sutcliffe urge leaders to create a "climate where people are wary of success, suspicious of quiet periods, and concerned about stability" and warn that just telling people to expect the unexpected isn't enough. Skilled bosses challenge their people to act with anticipation. Commercial pilots use a host of tricks to identify potential problems and think about how to deal with them no matter how normal things appear. JetBlue pilot and executive Bonny Warner-Simi tells me, "We incorporate this into our daily briefing. The key is to seek out what the threats might be. For example, a captain might say: 'I know the weather looks great, and we've all done this trip hundreds of times, but this can make us complacent. We need to be doubly careful.'"

Fight Right

Wise bosses like a good fight. A pile of studies show that when people fight over ideas, and do so with mutual respect, they are more productive and creative. The worst teams degenerate into nasty personal conflict, mercilessly insulting, teasing, and tearing each other down. Karl Weick captures the essence of a good argument: "Fight as if you are right, listen as if you are wrong." By pushing your ideas, pounding on others' ideas, and inviting others to pound on yours, too, the best ideas are formed and selected. If people can't fight without acting like assholes, it is better not to fight at all. But the best bosses ignite constructive battles over ideas. The list that follows gives tips for "How to Lead a Good Fight."

HOW TO LEAD A GOOD FIGHT

1. Don't begin the fight until everyone understands the challenge or problem at hand.

2. Don't argue while generating ideas or solutions—make it safe for people to suggest crazy or controversial ideas. After you have some ideas, then invite people to tear them apart.

3. If people turn nasty, take a time-out and ask them to turn off the venom. Pay special attention to comedians who deliver devastating insults via jokes and teasing.

4. Encourage everyone to argue. Gently silence people who talk too much and invite those who are silent to jump into the fray.

5. Don't just listen to people's words; watch their nonverbal behavior. Are they smiling? Really listening? Glaring, smirking, or rolling their eyes? Model constructive nonverbal behavior and coach people who (perhaps unwittingly) interject negative expressions.

6. Take special care to invite people who are shy, new, or at the bottom of the pecking order to express opinions—and defend them vigorously against personal attacks.

7. Learn people's quirks. Some have remarkably thick skins; nastiness doesn't faze them. Others are so thin-skinned that even gentle critiques send them into a rage or a funk.

8. Once the argument is resolved, make sure that the conflict and criticism ceases. It is time to develop and implement the agreed-upon ideas. Forbid people from rehashing complaints that "my great

idea" was killed and/or well-worn criticisms of "winning" ideas.

9. After the fight is over, do some backstage work. Soothe those who feel personally attacked and whose ideas were shot down. Give warnings and coaching to those who made personal attacks.

10. Despite mentoring and skilled facilitation, some people may prove to be too nasty or hypersensitive to criticism. You may need to exclude them from future battles, as their foibles may make it impossible for others to engage in constructive conflict.

Constructive confrontation has been used at Intel since the company was founded in 1968. All new hires take classes on how to do it. Intel employees tell me that these battles sometimes turn too nasty or too nice. In the hands of a skilled boss, however, these clashes produce remarkably well-vetted decisions—especially when people fight as equals over ideas. The best bosses forbid people from using political power, seniority, or expertise to bully others during such battles. The three-day sessions I described at *The Onion* follow similar rules. Although writers in their twenties work with Todd Hanson, an *Onion* writer for almost twenty years, they don't hesitate to shoot down his headlines—just as he shoots down theirs.

Brad Bird, Pixar's Academy Award–winning director, is a vigorous practitioner of creative abrasion. Bird explained to us that when he was hired to direct *The Incredibles*, executives Steve Jobs, Ed Catmull, and John Lasseter told him to challenge Pixar's status quo. Most companies bring in new blood because things are going badly. Pixar brought in the feisty and charming Bird after a string of blockbusters—starting with *Toy Story*—because they were worried that things were going *too* well. Bird's job was to crush complacency. They told him, "Go ahead, mess with our heads, shake it up." When Bird showed the Pixar technical team what he wanted in *The Incredibles*—difficult things like realistic hair, water, and fire—they "turned white" and warned it would take "take ten years and cost 500 million dollars." Bird challenged their assumptions with a team of "malcontents" who produced the film for under 100 million dollars:

> So I said, "Give us the black sheep. I want artists who are frustrated. I want the ones who have another way of doing things that nobody's listening to. Give us all the guys who are probably headed out the door." A lot of them were malcontents because they saw different ways of doing things, but there was little opportunity to try them, since the established way was working very, very well.

Bird's team clashed constantly and constructively while making *The Incredibles*. But Bird warned us that his experience elsewhere—notably directing *The Iron Giant*—taught him that good fights don't happen without hard-won trust. The *Iron Giant* team worked in a climate of fear before Bird arrived, which he worked to repair by telling them:

As individual animators, we all have different strengths and weaknesses, but if we can interconnect all our strengths, we are collectively the greatest animator on earth. So I want you guys to speak up and drop your drawers. We're going to look at your scenes in front of everybody. Everyone will get humiliated and encouraged together. If there is a solution, I want everyone to hear the solution, so everyone adds it to their tool kit. I'm going to take my shot at what I think will improve a scene, but if you see something different, go ahead and disagree. I don't know all the answers.

Bird's statement drips with wisdom: It shows how much people need each other and the virtues of exposing one's weaknesses. His line "Everyone will get humiliated and encouraged together" captures the essence of psychological safety.

Good bosses also know the wrong times to fight. Tearing apart a newborn idea can kill it before it develops enough to be judged. That is why skilled group brainstorming leaders forbid premature criticism. Argument and criticism are equally destructive once a team has decided which ideas to discard and which to keep and use. After a decision is made, whining on and on that your brilliant idea was superior to the idiotic final choice is risky because it saps everyone's energy for developing and implementing the winning ideas.

Sure, there are times when the best bosses stand their ground and fight on valiantly after a decision they believe is stupid has been made—and there are times when a boss is right to undermine the implementation of a rotten decision (and thus slow or limit the damage done). Before you engage in such resistance, however, remember that at the time a decision is made, it is usually impossible to know for sure if it is right or wrong (no matter how strongly you or others may oppose it). But you can be sure that even the best decision won't succeed unless people—even those who opposed it—work to implement it well. These facts of organizational life mean that it is often wisest to follow the eighth of TechRepublic's "Ten Commandments of Egoless Programming":

Fight for what you believe, but gracefully accept defeat. Understand that sometimes your ideas will be overruled. Even if you do turn out to be right, don't take revenge or say, "I told you so" more than a few times at most, and don't make your dearly departed idea a martyr or rallying cry.

Participation Traps

Wise bosses ask good questions, listen, and ask for help. But they don't expect followers to help them with every move or to participate in every decision. Too many well-meaning bosses fall into participation traps, involving people in too many decisions and the wrong decisions. In doing so, bosses often piss off their people and make it harder for them to do their work.

The first trap is creating unnecessary interference and distractions. As we will see in chapter 6, effective bosses shield people so they can do their work. Bosses who ask for too much input and assistance make it tough for people to concentrate. Michael Scott, the fictional bad boss on *The Office*, disrupted and distracted his Scranton group during one episode by asking his underlings to decide how to spend a $4,300 surplus. Rather than doing their jobs, they spent the day meeting, arguing, and campaigning over whether to spend it on a copier or chairs. *The Office* is fictional, but it triggered memories of real episodes in my academic life: I recall one painful meeting where two faculty members engaged in an inane and prolonged argument (while fifteen others were held hostage) about rules for using office supplies.

The second trap is that just because people can perform a job well doesn't mean they ought to help manage it. Asking employees to help bosses with their management chores is misguided when employees lack skill, interest, or time. The dangers of the first two traps (plus the virtues of participation) are seen in an intervention studied by Yale researcher Ingrid Nembhard and her colleagues. The goal was to increase communication and collaboration in twenty-three neonatal intensive care units (NICUs). These NICUs worked (to varying degrees) to involve front-line staff, including nurses, doctors, and respiratory therapists, in sharing information and making decisions. When people collaborated to improve care—such as controlling infections—lower mortality rates occurred among newborns in the NICUs. *But* getting frontline staff involved in managing these units was linked to higher mortality rates. In particular, when nurses participated in decisions like hiring, performance appraisals, salary setting, and budgeting, *more babies died!* This study examined a small sample of NICUs. But it ought to make even the most ardent advocates of employee participation think twice about its limitations. As Jeff Pfeffer puts it, the best bosses "let workers work."

The third trap is the most aggravating. I call it sham participation. It happens when the boss asks people to devote massive effort to help with some decision—serving on time-consuming committees, interviewing experts, preparing reports, and so on. But the boss knows from the outset that underlings will have no influence. Some bosses use sham participation in hopes of tricking powerless people into believing their input actually matters. Some believe it will persuade people to embrace rather than resist unpopular decisions. Others use it as window dressing, to persuade themselves and others they are benevolent and open-minded leaders, when they are nothing of the kind. I was recently reminded that no participation is better than sham participation by an angry e-mail from a European colleague who, after devoting many hours to a faculty committee that provided input on the design of a new building, was stunned when their advice was completely ignored. He was livid about the waste of time and disrespect: "Not one thing I said or argued for the whole time mattered." Every boss ought to learn a lesson from this pissed-off professor: sham participation is a sure-fire way to undermine people's productivity and wipe out their trust.

Deal with Your Achilles Heel

When people seem to be perfect, it just means you don't know them very well. A hallmark of wise bosses is that they are not only aware of their ignorance, weak skills, and character flaws—they actually do something about it. They deal with their Achilles' heels.

Wise people assume that their flaws aren't life sentences. They learn new skills and habits to overcome their weaknesses. After my father suffered a heart attack when I was a teenager, he joined a study group to reduce his type-A behavior. The researchers recruited type A's like my dad and taught them to tone down their hard-driving, impatient, and emotionally volatile behavior. The theory was that by mellowing out, participants would suffer fewer heart problems. I am not sure if the study helped others, but it helped my stereotypically type-A father become less tense and enjoy life more. One time I was driving with my dad and the stoplight ahead turned yellow. As usual, my dad floored it to race through the light. This time, however, he said, "Oh, shit,

I am not supposed to do that anymore." He then took a few deep breaths, and drove around the block slowly and returned to the intersection he had raced through—an exercise the researchers taught him to battle his "hurry sickness." My dad didn't exactly turn into Mr. Mellow, but my mother, sister, and I noticed that he calmed and slowed down a bit, as did the employees in his small company.

A related method is to recruit others to help you overcome your weaknesses. Consider the "Tape Method" used by Margie Mauldin, an executive coach in Denver. Margie told me about one of her clients, a government official who kept losing his temper at public meetings, alienating subordinates and the elected officials he served. As described on my blog, Work Matters, Margie went to meetings with her client and sat next to him. She brought a roll of duct tape. When he got up to speak, Margie used a four-step warning system:

1. At the first sign of excessive anger, she would take out the roll of tape and put it on the table next to him.
2. If he didn't calm down—or started getting even more irate—she would turn it on edge and roll it around a bit as a stronger reminder.
3. If he still was losing it—perhaps starting to pound the table, as he sometimes did—she would start peeling off a piece of tape and make sure he noticed she was doing it.

4. If all else failed, she would stand up and put a piece of tape over his mouth.

Margie never got to step 4 but reached step 3 quite a few times. She told me that this method worked because this client had a sense of humor and really wanted to stop his outbursts. After Margie used the Tape Method and other exercises that she devised, this official was able to reduce the frequency and severity of his outbursts.

Wise bosses also enlist followers as teachers. When Xerox promoted Anne Mulcahy to president and CEO heir apparent in 2000, the company was in a free fall, hemorrhaging money and facing accusations of financial impropriety. Mulcahy met with the top one hundred people in the company to listen to their concerns and ideas, and ask for their commitment to stick with her through the brutal turnaround ahead. She then went on an extensive fact-finding tour, visiting every major operation and listening to hundreds of customers and employees. Mulcahy also asked staff members to teach her more about finance, as she felt she needed to know more to do her job right. As she put it, "Folks in the controller's department would spend hours with me just making sure I was prepared to answer all the ugly, tough questions from bankers." Mulcahy became CEO in 2001, and Xerox returned to profitability in 2003. Xerox continued to have healthy profits through 2009 when Mulcahy retired as CEO and became the firm's chairman.

Wisdom: A Path to Empathy and Compassion

As we've seen, wise bosses get better performance from their people. But that is only part of the story. Wisdom bolsters their followers' humanity, too. When your boss listens to you carefully, reaches out to help you, and learns from you, it enhances your dignity and pride. Doing so also helps your boss gain empathy for you, to better understand how it feels to be you and what you need to succeed in your job and life.

These virtues of empathetic bosses are supported by a mountain of research. Recall the Swedish study showing that people with good, considerate bosses had fewer heart attacks. Gallup surveys show that employees with supervisors (or someone else) who care about them as people are happier and more committed to their work. The most striking lesson I ever had about wisdom and empathy came from Jim Plummer, my dean at Stanford. In 2004, I told Jim about a challenge facing my family. Our son, Tyler, has Asperger's syndrome, a condition related to autism that is manifested in social awkwardness and a lack of practical life skills. After an extensive search to find the right high school for Tyler (who was fourteen), my wife and I found that the best place was a long way from our family home and jobs. Our two daughters were ensconced in the local community and our jobs were nearby, so moving the whole family for those four years didn't make sense. To make our lives work, we needed to rent an apartment near the school and at the same time maintain our main family home near Stanford. And I would need to spend at least two nights a week at Tyler's apartment. One of my many worries about splitting our family was that to survive those years, my superiors at Stanford would need to give me permission to work a couple of days a week from the distant apartment.

When I talked to Jim about my challenge, he listened carefully (he always does). His first reaction was pure empathy: He could just as well be in my shoes. He talked about how his daughter (now a normal and healthy child) had been born prematurely and was at risk for a host of disabilities. Jim then asked questions about how I planned to satisfy teaching and research responsibilities during the coming years, acknowledged I was lucky to have a job where working at home so much was possible, and offered to write an e-mail supporting this arrangement. Tyler had a successful four years at the school, and although challenges remain ahead, he is a happy and increasingly independent adult. Getting through those years wasn't easy. But Jim's compassion and empathy was a lifeline I reached for in my mind almost every day during that time. As research on the best bosses suggests, Jim's warmth and understanding not only helped me feel dignity and pride about myself and my work—I also remain forever grateful to him.

The Attitude of Gratitude

Wise bosses don't just display empathy, compassion, and appreciation through dramatic and memorable gestures, as

Dean Plummer did for me. They convey it through tiny and seemingly trivial gestures. As we've seen, effective bosses work their magic by piling up one small win after another—and realizing that followers are watching their every move. A host of renowned bosses talk about the importance of thanking people, about the power of this small gesture, and how failure to express appreciation to people who are working their tails off is a sign of disrespect. The late Robert Townsend, former CEO of Avis Rent-a-Car and author of *Up the Organization*, defined "thanks" as "a really neglected form of compensation." Max DePree, former CEO of furniture giant Herman Miller, described saying "thank you" as among a leader's primary jobs. I thought all this talk about something so small and so obvious was overblown until a professor from another school told me about a trip he took with his university president to China. The logistics of the trip were difficult, as it was a traveling road show where transportation, hotel accommodations, meetings, and hundreds of other little details had to be orchestrated. The staff traveling with the group worked twelve to sixteen hours a day on these chores and did a magnificent job. Yet my colleague reported that even though the president made many requests of the staff during the trip, he never once thanked them. This lack of gratitude was demoralizing, as they catered to his every whim but weren't otherwise noticed or appreciated.

The broader lesson for bosses is that the attitude of wisdom is bolstered by "the attitude of gratitude." I borrowed this from Kimberly Wiefling, who argues that too many projects end without acknowledgement and celebration, and whether the project succeeded or failed, the best managers take a few hours to express appreciation. Expressing gratitude is especially important when the stench of failure is in the air. These are times when people most need support from the boss and each other. And doing so sets the stage for learning from the fiasco rather than for "blamestorms" or "circular fire squads," where the goal is to point fingers, humiliate the guilty, and throw a few overboard.

The attitude of wisdom isn't something that anyone learns all at once. Not even the best boss can achieve and sustain it every day and in every action. It is a mindset, a goal that one never achieves once and for all, an ongoing quest to strike the right balance between confidence and doubt, and between action and reflection. As we've seen, this mindset does, however, suggest concrete actions that bosses can take to spur performance and humanity. These actions are summarized in the accompanying "11 Commandments for Wise Bosses."

THE 11 COMMANDMENTS FOR WISE BOSSES

1. Have strong opinions and weakly held beliefs.
2. Do not treat others as if they are idiots.
3. Listen attentively to your people; don't just pretend to hear what they say.
4. Ask a lot of good questions.
5. Ask others for help and gratefully accept their assistance.

6. Do not hesitate to say, "I don't know."
7. Forgive people when they fail, remember the lessons, and teach them to everyone.
8. Fight as if you are right, and listen as if you are wrong.
9. Do not hold grudges after losing an argument. Instead, help the victors implement their ideas with all your might.
10. Know your foibles and flaws, and work with people who correct and compensate for your weaknesses.
11. Express gratitude to your people.

CHAPTER 4

Stars and Rotten Apples

In early 2008, I was reading *Fortune* magazine's list of the "100 Best Companies to Work for" and there, at #39, was Baird, a privately held Midwest company. *Fortune* explained, "What makes it so great? They tout the 'no-a**hole rule' at this financial services firm; candidates are interviewed extensively, even by assistants who will be working with them." Executives at other companies on the list that year, including #1 Google, told me they applied the rule, too. But only Baird identified it as the central theme. I immediately contacted Leslie Dixon, their HR chief. Leslie was effusive as she explained Baird's policy and culture, and arranged a conversation with CEO Paul Purcell.

Paul reported he had seen and suffered destructive assholes in past jobs, so when he got to Baird, he vowed to build a jerk-free workplace. When I asked how he enforced the rule, Paul said that most jerks were screened out via background checks and interviews before they met him. But he did his own filtering, too: "During the interview, I look them in the eye and tell them, 'If I discover that you are an asshole, I am going to fire you.'" He added, "Most candidates aren't fazed by this, but every now and then, one turns pale, and we never see them again— they find some reason to back out of the search." When I asked Paul what kinds of jerks are most poisonous, he said: "The worst assholes consistently do two things: (1) Put themselves ahead of clients and (2) put themselves ahead of the company or their colleagues." Paul's approach seems to be working, as Baird moved up to #13 on *Fortune*'s list in 2009 and then to #11 in 2010. Despite the troubled financial services industry, Baird's revenue and profits continued to be strong through 2008 and 2009 and, while other firms in the industry were downsizing, their workforce grew by six percent in 2009. As *Fortune* reported in 2010, Baird continued to screen talent "via rigorous interviews to ensure that they passed the firm's 'no asshole' rule." Certainly, Paul wants people with magnificent skills for jobs in, say, financial services, human resources, or sales. But he wants more: people who make a positive rather than negative impact on others' performance and humanity.

As former U.S. Supreme Court Justice Sandra Day O'Connor put it, "We don't accomplish anything in this world alone...and whatever happens is the result of the whole tapestry of one's life and all the weavings of individual threads from one to another that creates something." The best bosses don't just recruit people with stellar solo skills; they bring in employees who will weave their vigor and talents with others. Such "connective talents" are less crucial when people work largely unfettered by coworkers, such as long-haul truckers or solo salespeople. Yet even then, no man or woman is an island. Truckers, for example, deal with management, warehouses, and fellow truckers—so they must play well with others, too. This need for connective talents extends to distributed teams and networks, where members spread across the continent or globe coordinate via phone calls, e-mails, video, and perhaps an occasional face-to-face meeting. Many dispersed teams and networks do work that requires precise orchestration of ideas and actions, like designing software systems for SAP, designing and building planes for Boeing, building cars for Ford, and carrying out U.S. military operations.

Interdependence is an inescapable and necessary fact of organizational life. But it still drives most of us crazy at times. The resulting entanglements condemn us to endure each other's quirks, intrusions, annoying habits, clashing opinions, petty demands, and pathetic incompetence—and force others to endure our imperfections in return. Jean-Paul Sartre was right when he said, "Hell is just other people"; but bosses need people who can excel in such hell. People who can't or won't play well with others drag down performance. And if you insist on bringing aboard socially challenged, excessively competitive, or nasty people (or are stuck with some) you need to find ways to limit the damage.

Connective talents are useless, of course, if people can't perform the work. And the most talented people in every occupation have huge advantages over their ordinary peers. Dean Keith Simonton, who studies greatness and genius, finds that whether it comes to songwriters, composers, scientists, programmers, or filmmakers, the top 10 percent generate as much or more output than the other 90 percent. The superiority of great bosses is seen in a summary of eighty-five years of research on employee selection methods. Frank Schmidt and John Hunter found that the top 15 percent of professionals and managers produced nearly 50 percent more output than their average peers. The strongest predictors of performance included general mental ability (IQ and similar measures), job sample tests (having people prove they can do the work), and evaluations by peers; other useful predictors included structured employment interviews (where each candidate is asked the same questions in the same order) and conscientiousness (self-discipline and follow-through, similar to grit).

These findings provide ammunition for bosses who stock up on the best talent and believe that little else is required. Yet without constructive connections among people, collective performance and humanity is tough to achieve—no matter how many superstars are in the fold. As Paul Purcell argues, talented employees who put their needs ahead of their colleagues and the company are dangerous. An episode at the retailer Men's Wearhouse shows the hazards of selfish stars—and virtues of expelling them.

Charles O'Reilly and Jeff Pfeffer tell us, "the company fired one of its top-producing salespeople because he stole other people's sales and didn't buy into the company's values and philosophy. Although no one in that store subsequently sold as much as the person who had been fired, total stores sales went up almost 30 percent. That one individual brought the others down, and when he was gone, they could do their best."

This chapter shows how bosses can select and breed employees who not only produce splendid solo performances, but bring out the best (rather than the worst) in others, too.

Who Are Your Stars?

That is the first question I ask when a boss has performance problems, is plagued by caustic conflict, or is losing good people at an alarming rate. I want to know if the anointed stars enhance or undermine others' performance and humanity. Unfortunately, too many bosses have such blind faith in solo superstars and unbridled competition that they hire egomaniacs and install pay and promotion systems that reward selfish creeps who don't give a damn about their colleagues. Or, even worse, they shower kudos and cash on credit hogs and back-stabbers who get ahead by knocking others down. As researcher Morten Hansen shows, when this happens, selfish "lone stars" breed like rabbits and rule the roost. And while stunning solo performances may occur, collaboration and cooperation evaporate, and so do collective innovation and performance.

This toxic brew starts—or can end—during the hiring process. I once worked with a successful and civilized law firm that brought in consultants to help them increase profits. They were already ranked among the one hundred most profitable law firms in the United States, and profits were steadily increasing. The consultants offered advice that still floors me: They were concerned that these lawyers were too nice and cooperative and urged the firm to recruit some "BSDs," which stands for "Big Swinging Dicks": hard-charging, rather nasty, and selfish rainmakers with big books of business and a "take no prisoners" attitude. The consultants reasoned that hiring BSDs wouldn't just increase the firm's profits, it would increase competition among partners, toughen them up, and drive out those ill suited to play the rough new game. The firm's leaders politely dismissed the idea because importing a band of BSDs would have destroyed their culture. These bosses didn't want a hypercompetitive firm like the one "Henry" led where, as described earlier, "We used to pride ourselves for having the best balance of humanity and economics in the business. Under Henry's leadership, it is all economics all the time, humanity be damned." You won't be surprised to learn that Henry bragged about the BSDs he hired from other firms.

The problem with treating work as an "I win, you lose" game isn't just that it makes things so unpleasant. As we saw at the Men's Wearhouse, it undermines performance.

Unfortunately, many bosses who pay lip service to cooperation unwittingly implement reward systems that stomp it out. They fall prey to what Steve Kerr called "the Folly of Rewarding A, While Hoping for B": They use reward systems that encourage selfishness every day and in every way, while hoping that people will play well with others. The defunct Merrill Lynch (now part of Bank of America) used a pay system that demonstrates this folly. In *Riding the Bull*, Paul Stiles describes what it was like to be a new trader at the firm. During his first weeks, Stiles asked for advice and tips from seasoned traders. They largely ignored him because their bonuses were based solely on individual financial performance; every minute they spent mentoring Stiles cost them money. As Dan and Chip Heath tell it, "Eventually, Stiles was reduced to silently observing their behavior from a distance, like a rogue MBA anthropologist. It surely never dawned on the person who set up Merrill Lynch's incentive system that the traders' bonuses would make training new employees impossible."

Merrill stuck with this system until the bitter end. But some organizations—and bosses—learn about the hazards of overglorifying solo stars. One of my graduate students was on an engineering team renowned for its creativity. The team was assigned a new boss who believed that injecting competition would propel them to even more impressive feats. He started paying individuals a modest bonus for each idea they generated during group brainstorms or e-mailed to him. He paired these modest incentives with a large bonus for ideas that ultimately were used in the company's products. Before this system was implemented, brainstorms were rollicking and noisy, routinely producing a hundred or more ideas in less than sixty minutes. After the change, the engineers rarely generated even a dozen ideas during these gatherings. Before, no one cared much who got credit for ideas. Afterwards, engineers insisted—when they proposed an idea—that their initials be placed next to it on the whiteboard. These engineers had once spent their days talking openly about ideas, bouncing them off one another, and blending them in new ways. Under the new system, things devolved quickly—rather than going to lunch together as in the past, each ate alone in his cubicle. The boss finally abandoned the system after devoting most of a brainstorm to arguing with two engineers about which one deserved credit for an idea. When he insisted on giving them both credit, they degenerated into a debate over which of the two deserved more credit. None of the engineers complained when the boss announced the system was a flop and would be terminated. Slowly, over several months, their old, constructive patterns returned.

Harry S. Truman said, "It is amazing what you can accomplish if you do not care who gets the credit." That is a lovely sentiment and a useful worldview—to a point. Some people are usually more crucial to collective success than others and arguably deserve a larger share of the goodies. And when bosses make no effort to differentiate people who make constructive contributions from those who do not, losers who bring down the team get off scot-free or, worse yet, are rewarded.

There are two ways that skilled bosses deal with this challenge. The first is by selecting and promoting people with a track record of cooperative and selfless acts. This is what they do at Baird by screening out (and firing) assholes who put their needs and wants ahead of coworkers and the firm. In the same spirit, A. G. Lafley, former CEO of Procter & Gamble, reports that P&G doesn't use fancy pay schemes to reward cooperation, rather, "managers who fail to share ideas simply do not get promoted."

The second way was explained to me by a group of General Electric executives a few years back. I pressed them about their rather extreme "rank and yank" system (which has been modified recently, but not much), where each year the bottom 10 percent of employees ("C players") are fired, the top 20 percent ("A players") get the lion's share—about 80 percent—of the bonus money, and the mediocre middle 70 percent ("B players") get the remaining crumbs. I pressed them because a pile of studies shows that giving a few top performers most of the goodies damages team and organizational performance. This happens because people have no incentive to help others—but do have an incentive to undermine, bad-mouth, and demoralize coworkers, because pushing down others decreases the competition they face. Performance also suffers because hard workers who aren't anointed A players become bitter and withhold effort. The GE executives answered that yes, these problems occurred, but they eliminated many by defining A players as those who did great solo work *and* helped colleagues and businesses succeed. That way, only cooperative people were crowned as A players, so all the B players they helped were less likely to resent the differentiation.

When I looked more closely at places where people were cooperative and unselfish, I saw that although their reward systems varied wildly, they all applied something like the GE definition of a superstar. Examples include biotechnology firm Genencor, renowned Berkeley restaurant Chez Panisse, IDEO, Google, McKinsey, Procter & Gamble, and Southwest Airlines. Morten Hansen shows that organizations like these promote innovation and effectiveness through "the power of two performances": individual contributions on their own jobs and collaboration on and across teams.

In short, if you are a boss, ask yourself: "Who have I anointed as stars?" Think of your workplace more broadly and ask, "Do we anoint people who bolster or bring down others' performance and humanity?" To help answer these questions, complete the twenty-item survey at the end of this chapter: the EGOS, or "Evaluation Gauge for Obnoxious Superstars." The EGOS can give you a quick (if nonscientific) reading on whether your workplace is best described as "kill or be killed," "help others succeed or get the hell out," or somewhere in between.

Bring on the Energizers

Rob Cross studies social networks: how information, ideas, and influence travel through the web of relationships that compose every team and organization. A few years back, Rob and his colleagues were designing a survey to map the connections among employees within several big companies. They wanted to identify what kinds of employees were top performers and brought out the best in others. They hypothesized that people who were renowned for having expertise, spreading technical knowledge, and best positioned to gather and weave together information from others would be seen as top performers. At a professional services firm they were studying, an executive argued they were missing something:

> We have some of the brightest consultants in the world here. But some are more successful than others, and it has much more to do with what I call buzz than a slight difference in IQ. Our high performers create enthusiasm for things.... They create energy, and even though this is intangible it generates client sales and follow-on work as well as gets other people here engaged in and supportive of what they are doing.

Inspired by this insight, they added a simple question to their survey: "People can affect the energy and enthusiasm we have at work in various ways. Interactions with some people can leave you feeling drained while others can leave you feeling enthused about possibilities. When you interact with each person below, how does it typically affect your energy level?" The possible answers were: 1 = de-energizing;

2 = no effect/neutral; or 3 = energizing. The colleagues in their team or business were then listed, and each was rated by every coworker.

Rob and his fellow researchers were stunned by how strongly this "energy" question predicted performance evaluations and promotions, and whether people stayed with or left an organization. They also found that the most successful teams and organizations had networks filled with interconnected energizers. Cross and his colleagues have since dug into the kinds of people who are energizers and why they succeed. "Energizers" aren't necessarily charismatic and bubbly; on the surface, many are understated and rather shy. But all create energy via optimism about the possibilities ahead, fully engaging the person right in front of them right now, valuing others' ideas, and helping people feel as if they are making progress.

The late Gordon MacKenzie held a position at Hallmark Cards as "the Creative Paradox." MacKenzie was a successful designer, led innovative design teams, and taught inspiring creativity workshops to everyone from kindergarteners to CEOs. In *Orbiting the Giant Hairball,* MacKenzie described how he sparked positive energy when he was Hallmark's Creative Paradox:

> I became a liaison between the chaos of creativity and the discipline of business. I had no job description and a title that made no sense, but people started coming to me with their ideas, and I would listen to those ideas and validate them. When you validate a person,

what you're really doing is giving them power—like a battery charger.

Again, energizers don't need to be bubbly or exciting. When I think of a soft-spoken energizer, Lenny Mendonca comes to mind, a partner at McKinsey who has held senior positions including head of the strategy practice and chair of the McKinsey Global Institute. Before I met Lenny, my stereotype of McKinsey partners was they were smooth-talking egomaniacs. Lenny is exactly the opposite. I remember a great dinner that my colleague Hayagreeva "Huggy" Rao and I had with Lenny at the Half Moon Bay Brewing Company (which Lenny owns). Huggy and I were touched by how encouraging and constructive Lenny had been about research we were pursuing. Huggy, an astute observer, pointed out how closely Lenny listened, how he saw possible value in every person and every idea and—unlike the two of us—rarely interrupted. Huggy and I are just two of Lenny's fans; he has the same energizing effect on everyone who knows him.

Rotten Apples: Bad Is Stronger Than Good

Unfortunately, accentuating the positive isn't enough. The best bosses do more than charge up people, and recruit and breed energizers. They eliminate the *negative*, because even a few bad apples and destructive acts can undermine many good people and constructive acts. The case for reforming or, failing that, expelling the worst offenders is bolstered by Will Felps's research on "bad apples." Felps and his colleagues studied what I call *dead-beats* ("withholders of effort"), *downers* (who "express pessimism, anxiety, insecurity, and irritation," a toxic breed of de-energizer), and *assholes* (who violate "interpersonal norms of respect"). Felps estimates that teams with just one deadbeat, downer, or asshole suffer a performance disadvantage of 30 to 40 percent compared to teams that have no bad apples.

These rotten apples are so destructive because "bad is stronger than good." For most people, negative thoughts, feelings, and events produce larger and longer-lasting effects than positive ones. Research on romantic relationships shows that unless positive interactions outnumber negative interactions by five to one, chances the relationship will succeed are slim. When the proportion of negative interactions exceeds this "five-to-one rule," marital satisfaction goes way down and the divorce rate goes way up. Similarly, a study that tracked employees' moods found that the impact of negative interactions with bosses and coworkers on employees' feelings were five times stronger than positive interactions. Negative interactions (and the bad apples who provoke them) pack such a wallop in close relationships because they are so distracting, emotionally draining, and deflating. When a group does interdependent work, rotten apples drag down and infect everyone else. Unfortunately, grumpiness, nastiness, laziness, and stupidity are remarkably contagious.

The upshot is that as a boss, you can't wait very long to see if these destructive characters will mend their ways. You need to intervene quickly. If pointed and persistent feedback fails, do everything you can to expel the bad apple. A few years back, I was teaching student teams working with Wal-Mart to help frontline employees become more aware of the environmental impact of the products they sold. The project had tight deadlines and a high-pressure presentation for executives. One team complained that a member had missed most meetings and wasn't doing any work. When I talked to him, he admitted to "blowing off" his team because he was busy interviewing for a Rhodes Scholarship and a job at Google—but insisted he was so talented that he deserved to stay on the team. This student thought he was so smart that he didn't need to do any work. But he was just a rotten apple. He dropped the class once I convinced him he was headed for a lousy grade. The team went on to do wonderful work, and the deadbeat did not get the Rhodes Scholarship or the Google job.

Other Smart People Tricks

1. Show Them the Love

Organizational life is filled with time-consuming and distracting routines that burden every boss. In the crush of satisfying deadlines, going to meetings, and plowing through red tape, more important things can fall through the cracks. Exhibit #1 is performance evaluations. Many organizations

impose such rigid, legalistic, inhuman, and onerous evaluation procedures that these chores distract bosses from tend-
ing to their followers in more important ways. I've worked
with and been part of too many places where bosses spend
endless hours preparing evaluations but don't take even a
few moments to make people feel appreciated.

Joel Podolny is the boss who taught me the power of
showing a little love. Joel is a former dean of the Yale School
of Management and currently an Apple vice president and
dean of their internal "University." I knew Joel as an associate
dean at the Stanford Business School, where he did a master-
ful job. Joel is the only academic dean I've ever met who
wandered the halls several times a week, talking to faculty
about what they were doing and the challenges they faced.
Joel had thousands of things to do, but he always took time
to listen to and show appreciation to the faculty he served.
Joel was well loved because he was so empathetic and unselfish; he automatically made decisions and expressed emotions
best for the person in front of him (and the institution).

I was especially impressed with Joel's approach when a
faculty member asked for a raise and threatened to move to
another university—a routine part of any dean's job. Joel told
me something like "I always get to the money eventually, but
when a faculty member is talking about leaving they often
aren't feeling sufficiently appreciated, so I start out by telling
them how much I love and appreciate them and all the ways
that their colleagues do, too. After we work through that, I
turn to the money. It nearly always turns out that the love
and appreciation issue is bigger than the money." Bosses in

hundreds of occupations can learn from Joel—spend less time on those endless routine chores (perhaps do a half-assed job on some that don't matter much) and spend more time showing your people a little love.

2. Assume the Best

Joel's story highlights that too many bosses forget the power of the human touch, which also entails conveying confidence to followers. The power of believing that good things will happen to your people, and communicating that to them—the self-fulfilling prophecy—is supported by much research. Consider a study of drill instructors at an Army boot camp. In this field experiment with Israeli soldiers, five drill instructors were tricked by researchers into believing that ten of the thirty soldiers that each would lead for the next fifteen weeks was nearly certain to achieve superior performance. The researchers told the drill instructors that based on past research, they could predict a soldier's command potential ("CP") with 95 percent accuracy. But the researchers were lying and had actually randomly selected the "stars." The drill instructors were told these lies just once at the start of the course via the following instruction:

> You will copy each trainee's CP into his personal record. You are requested to learn your trainees' names and their predicted CP by the beginning of the course. Please copy the names and predictions into the records now.

This tiny intervention lasted only a few minutes but packed a wallop over the next fifteen weeks. Those randomly anointed soldiers were treated differently by instructors and came to believe they had special talents. During the course, there were huge differences between the anointed soldiers and everyone else. They displayed superior performance on many tasks, including firing weapons and reading maps. This study shows how the self-fulfilling prophecy works: the drill instructors believed something that was, at first, untrue, but believing it caused them to transform those lies into truths.

Studies on the self-fulfilling prophecy demonstrate that believing in *some* of your people can boost their performance. But my students always ask: "Do you need a group of both winners and losers? What if a boss believes that everyone is great?" Fortunately, there seems to be no need to mix winners and losers; follow-up studies by the "boot camp" researchers show that when a drill instructor believes all soldiers have high command potential, all perform better. The upshot is that smart bosses can spark performance by expressing confidence (in fact, overconfidence) in all their people. Southwest Airlines uses this technique: one of the first things that they tell new hires— in a large group setting—is that they are the "cream, cream, cream of the crop."

The self-fulfilling prophecy isn't a sure cure. Pygmalion effects are stronger in military organizations than in businesses, apparently because superiors have more frequent and intense interactions with followers. The prophecy is also sometimes not fulfilled because even if the boss believes and acts as if followers are destined for greatness, contrary actions by fellow bosses, customers, and co-workers can undermine the message. Yet believing your people can and will perform splendidly creates better results than doubting their ability or believing they are losers.

3. Cut Loose the Real Losers

The self-fulfilling prophecy doesn't always work. You can bring in people who seem like talented stars, devote massive attention to them, and give them every chance to succeed. Yet their performance may still suck. The challenge for bosses—as for all human beings—is that they see what they believe. Psychologists call this confirmation bias: selective thinking where "one tends to notice and to look for what confirms one's beliefs, and to ignore, not look for, or undervalue the relevance of what contradicts one's beliefs." As Simon and Garfunkel put it in their song "The Boxer," "a man hears what he wants to hear and disregards the rest." This happens to women, too.

Confirmation bias can cause bosses to make excessively glowing judgments about people they have invested a lot of time and money in or who they simply find to be likable or admirable. Even if your judgment is generally sound, confirmation bias can blind you to mediocre or even downright rotten performance displayed by your favorites. Barry Staw and Ha Hoang tracked players taken in the college draft by teams in the National Basketball Association—where teams pick players they believe are most talented in early rounds and those believed to be less talented in later rounds. Over a six-year stretch—*regardless of their objective performance*—players picked earlier in the draft (those thought to be more talented) were given more playing time, were less likely to be traded to other teams, and had longer careers than peers picked in later rounds (and thus thought to be less talented).

NBA coaches and officials responded to Staw and Hoang that they couldn't possibly make such irrational decisions because so much money was at stake and they were so committed to winning. They were wrong. Irrational commitment to an anointed star who is really a loser can happen to any boss, no matter how experienced they are or how high the stakes. If you are worried this is happening to you, try looking at performance data without names attached to the numbers (if you can get them), or bring in an unbiased outsider to help you judge your people.

4. Keep Teams Together

Bringing in people with connective talents and celebrating stars that help others succeed are powerful means for accomplishing interdependent work. But even if you get the best people and put them in the best system, learning to work together takes time. Consider the first U.S. women's national soccer team, which won numerous championships, including two of the first four Women's World Cups and two of the first three Olympic women's tournaments. They had talented players like Mia Hamm, Brandi Chastain, Julie Foudy, and Joy Fawcett. But the key to their success—as all will tell you—was that a tight-knit and stable group was the heart and soul of the team for a dozen years or so. It takes time for people to learn each other's strengths and weaknesses and develop effective shared ways of doing things.

Evidence for the virtues of "hard teams," "team stability," or "prior joint experience" comes from many settings, including leadership teams, surgical teams, product development groups, and airplane cockpit crews. One study tracked 98 (of the 102) semiconductor firms founded in the United States between 1978 and 1985. The researchers discovered that when a founding team's members had worked together before, companies enjoyed greater financial success in the first two years and this advantage kept getting stronger in subsequent years. Even a little experience together helps: In 1994, the National Transportation Safety Board reported that 73 percent of the mistakes made during commercial airline flights happened during the first twenty-four hours of the (typically) seventy-two-hour stint that a cockpit crew spent together. They also found that 44 percent of these errors happen on the crew's first flight together.

Eventually, teams need new blood to bring in different ideas. But it takes longer for them to go stale than you might think. A study of R&D teams with stable membership found that they got more and more productive during their first four years or so, but productivity finally started dropping if they did not bring in new members after about five years.

5. Protect Yourself from the Energy Suckers

Part of being the boss is that when something bad happens, or someone is unhappy, it is your job to deal with it. Yet, as the research shows, the more time you spend around rotten apples—those lousy, lazy, grumpy, and nasty people—the more damage you will suffer. When people are emotionally depleted, they stop focusing on their jobs and instead work on improving their moods. If you find that there are a few subordinates who are so unpleasant that, day after day, they sap the energy you need to inspire others and feel good about your own job, my advice—if you can't get rid of them—is to spend as little time around them as possible. An executive from the Midwest once told me about a senior engineer at his firm who was admired for his ability to spot flaws, but was widely feared and despised for being "100 percent mean." No matter the occasion—the review of a drawing or an all-hands meeting—he not only ripped ideas apart, he ripped people apart, including his bosses. Senior management believed he was too valuable to fire, so they moved him to a nice private office in a different building that was blocks away. That way, his superiors and peers could avoid as much incidental contact with him as possible.

Most bosses can't place such energy suckers in splendid isolation. When you can't avoid them, just work on not letting them get under your skin. I've urged people who work for nasty bosses to practice the art of emotional detachment, so those creeps wouldn't touch their souls. Similar advice holds for bosses: If you can't escape the deadbeats, downers, and assholes you supervise, go through the required motions to manage them, but train yourself to care less about them and their destructive ways. Save your passion and creativity for those people who will benefit from it and who leave you feeling charged up rather than drained. Developing the fine art of indifference and emotional detachment is part of becoming a boss with grit. If you believe that you are running a marathon rather than a sprint, you can't let the unavoidable and unpleasant parts of the race undermine your progress toward long-term goals.

6. When to Divide and Conquer

This chapter focuses on work that requires cooperation and coordination. As I said at the outset, connective social talents are less essential when people do work that requires little contact and coordination with others. Going a step further, some bosses lead individuals who lack connective skills and have no interest in dealing with others. If you lead such lone wolves, and their skills are impossible to replace, the best solution might be to design their work so that you coordinate and weave their tasks together and your charges are left to work pretty much alone.

A manager in a semiconductor company once explained

to me why this "divide and conquer" strategy was the only way to deal with the talented but reclusive engineers in his firm:

> They hide in their offices, and don't come out. We divide the work so they each have a separate part. We slide their assignments under the door and run away. They ignore us when we tell them it is good enough—they won't let us build it until it meets their standards for elegant designs—they don't care what we think.

These engineers lacked connective talents and had little interest in dealing with others. But rather than trying to change them, management built a system where engineers had no need to deal with peers, and bosses took the responsibility for dividing up and blending their efforts. This isn't the path to a warm and fuzzy workplace. But there are times when the "divide and conquer" strategy is the best a boss can do.

Take a Look in the Mirror

All bosses have limited power over who they lead, how people are rewarded, who chooses to stay, and which followers they can expel. Yet even when bosses face scarce resources and cumbersome work rules, and have limited authority, there are still vast differences between the best and worst. Author and consultant Wally Bock saw the impact of such differences when he worked to identify and develop effective sergeants in the Oakland Police Department in the 1980s. Wally was especially impressed with Sgt. John Ludden. He was widely admired by fellow officers for treating each with respect, not playing favorites, and always, always being on their side.

John's reputation meant that officers wanted to work with him. As Wally told me, "Officers with more time with the department and more time at their rank got to pick the shift they wanted to work ahead of those with less time." When John was a new sergeant, he got the graveyard shift, from 11:00 PM to 7:00 AM: "Normally that would mean that his squad would be 100 percent rookies. But some senior officers volunteered to work on John's squad, even though they could have picked a better shift, because they wanted to work with John."

John Ludden's story is bolstered by the research outlined in chapter 1 and many other studies: Good bosses don't just get more out of their people and do it in more civilized ways; they attract and keep better people. The implication is that if the people you lead are mired in dysfunctional competition, and you are surrounded with energy suckers, deadbeats, downers, and assholes, take a look in the mirror. Why don't the best people want to work for you? Why do people who seemed to be stars when they joined your team often seem to turn rotten? As Wally's work suggests, if this is your predicament, take a close look at what the best bosses in your line of work do, face the facts about what you do differently, and start closing the gap.

EGOS SURVEY (EVALUATION GAUGE FOR OBNOXIOUS SUPERSTARS)

Are You Hiring and Breeding Greedy and Selfish Employees?

Answer true or false to each statement below. The people who get ahead at my workplace:

1. say "we" but think "me."
2. see their peers as competitors, even "the enemy."
3. remove subordinates' names from good work before passing it up the chain.
4. belittle others' triumphs and successes.
5. hoard their ideas because, after all, there is no reward for sharing them with colleagues.
6. are chronic credit hogs.
7. stomp on others on the way to the top.
8. often ask for help from colleagues but rarely return the favor.
9. are world-class backstabbers, remarkably adept at destroying the reputations of peers, subordinates, and bosses whom they see as competitors.
10. stockpile resources and won't share, no matter how badly others need them.
11. routinely rip apart colleagues—not just their ideas, but their reputations and self-confidence, too.
12. are such all-star ass-kissers that their superiors adore them, but they are despised by peers and subordinates.
13. negotiate for more and more goodies for themselves but never go to bat for others.

14. conveniently "forget" to invite colleagues to high-profile meetings.
15. do what is best for themselves first and rarely what is best for their team or the organization.
16. say nice things to their bosses' faces but rip them to shreds behind their backs.
17. don't waste time teaching or mentoring others.
18. are black holes of information: it only goes in, never out to colleagues.
19. insist on being "in the loop" but don't return the favor.
20. live the *30 Rock* mantra—"I'm going to get mine!"

Scoring the EGOS: Add up the number of statements that you marked as true. This isn't a scientifically validated test, but here is how I would describe your workplace:

0 to 4: **Help others succeed or get the hell out.** If you are telling the truth, your workplace selects and breeds unselfish stars, and reforms (or drives out) selfish creeps.

5 to 10: **Help others succeed, but watch your back.** Your workplace is at the borderline between anointing collaborative versus selfish stars. People collaborate and there are rewards for doing so, but enough selfish behavior happens that anointed stars grab goodies and credit for themselves and protect themselves against getting screwed—especially by their most selfish and devious coworkers.

11 to 15: **Watch out for number one, otherwise you are screwed.** Your people are playing a competitive, "I win, you lose" game every day. Selfishness and backstabbing abound, and collaborators are crushed by the system. Even the most naturally cooperative people learn to

become selfish and do a bit of backstabbing in such places, otherwise survival is impossible.

16 to 20: **Kill or be killed.** You are in a dog-eat-dog world where the only way for people to get ahead is to treat their coworkers as enemies and to crush their spirits and reputations every chance they get. No one lasts long in such a place without becoming an overbearing and selfish jerk who screws colleagues at every turn.

CHAPTER 5

Link Talk and Action

The "smart-talk trap" happens when bosses and their people know what needs to be done and keep talking about it, writing about it, studying it—yet all that blabbering becomes an end in itself rather than a stepping stone to action. Somehow, the pile of words (and numbers and pictures) generated via glib talk, brainstorming sessions, protracted arguments, presentations, strategic planning, stage gates, scenario planning, board meetings, mission statements, budgets, and sales forecasts can be weirdly comforting even when it has no impact on what people actually need to do to succeed. Consider a few examples:

- A restaurant chain paid a consulting firm several million dollars to develop a detailed plan to improve their operations. As the consultants presented their report, a veteran executive commented that the company had bought pretty much the same report a decade earlier from other consultants. He then read passage after passage from the old report, which contained virtually the same advice as the new report. Senior management had known what to do for a long time: their organization just hadn't done it.

- A vice president in a troubled retail chain complained to me about his weekly meetings with fellow executives: "I feel like I've been going to the same meeting for twenty-five years; we talk about the same problems, come up with the same solutions, and pretend that by talking about what should happen, it actually will—but somehow it never does."

- I asked Pixar's two-time Academy Award–winner Brad Bird: What kind of people are especially poisonous to innovation? He answered: "People who talk quality but don't put it in their own work, yeah, it's those types. You know, I don't mind somebody who's green if they're engaged, because I know they're on the hunt. But there are people who know the buzzwords of quality people, but don't actually walk the walk."

- Elizabeth Gerber and I asked student teams to brainstorm and implement ways to improve bike safety on the Stanford campus. They had forty-eight hours to do the assignment. Bike accidents are common at Stanford because students zip around blind corners, weave through crowds, and race downhill—often while yakking on cell phones. One team used orange cones and yellow tape to construct a bicycle roundabout at a crossroads plagued with collisions, known as "the intersection of death." The roundabout took about thirty minutes to set up and worked remarkably well during a two-hour test. Stanford police officers stumbled upon the team and pitched in to help build the prototype: They loved how well it worked. The good news is there is now a permanent concrete roundabout at the intersection of death; the bad news is it took about four years to install it. Elizabeth traced the roundabout's history. When she asked a university official why it took so long, he became defensive and argued that he had the idea long before the students ever tried it. If this official knew it before, why wasn't it implemented—or at least tested—earlier?

- "Respect: We treat others as we would like to be treated ourselves. Ruthlessness, callousness and arrogance don't belong here." And "Integrity: We work with customers and prospects openly, honestly and sincerely." These are excerpts from Enron's sixty-four-page "Code of Ethics."

Jeff Pfeffer and I wrote about such maladies in *The Knowing-Doing Gap* ten years ago, and we have since explored causes and cures with bosses of all kinds, ranging from ministers, to chefs, to executives in the National Football League, to CEOs of nonprofits, tiny start-ups, and Fortune 500 companies. Bosses of every stripe recognize the smart-talk trap immediately, tell us stories about it, and point to impediments that make it tough for them to avoid it. Even the best bosses sometimes fail to implement good ideas—the knowing-doing gap is an inescapable fact of organizational life. Yet there are striking differences between the worst and the best. The worst don't even realize that they routinely stifle and misdirect action. The best find ways to close knowing-doing gaps, even in workplaces otherwise plagued by hollow talk and inaction. Here is how good bosses close the gap.

Don't Be a Clueless Blabbermouth—Or Let Them Rule the Roost

As a boss, you need to establish a pecking order where people who know the most about a problem wield the greatest influence over what is done. You especially need to watch who talks the most (and least). Don't let your people fall prey to the blabbermouth theory of leadership. At least in Western countries, people who talk first and most frequently usually wield excessive influence over others—even when they spew out nonsense. And, regardless of personality, when people are granted power over others (including just placing them at the head of a table), they start talking more and ordering people around. As we saw in chapter 3, some bosses make this problem worse by rambling on and stifling underlings, and insisting they are right even when they are dead wrong.

Matthew May describes a dirty trick that he played on a group of General Motors (GM) executives to show them how their pecking order produced bad decisions. Matt knows his stuff: He has extensive experience in writing about and consulting with the auto industry. Here is the story that Matt posted on my blog:

I was doing some consulting with a division of GM and told them the best ideas were not getting heard—in fact, no ideas were being heard. The managers told me that wasn't true. During an offsite, I had the opportunity to design part of the program. It was an age-old prioritization game called Survival on the Moon: You've crashed landed on the moon, 200 clicks from the mother ship, with 25 items you have to rank in the order of their importance in surviving the trek to the ship. You do it individually, then as a group, in order to make the point that "we" is smarter "me." (There is a right order, provided by NASA.) I constructed the table rounds cross-hierarchically, so one table might have a VP and a lowly staffer. Then I played a dirty trick: I gave the lowest ranking person at each table the answers ahead of time, saying that when it came time for the group ranking, their job was to do everything in their power to convince the table they had the right ranking, short of revealing that I had given them the answer. Not a single table (about 15 tables of 10 people) got the right answer. Then I had the ringers stand up. Got to catch all the managers red-faced.

In other words, even though Matt instructed those underlings to do everything possible to convince the alpha dogs they knew the right answers, they were ignored and muzzled. These groups had the knowledge to do the right thing but couldn't do it because of their defective pecking orders. Good bosses are keenly aware that people who know the most are sometimes the least vocal and pushy. As Nolan Bushnell, founder of Atari (an early computer game company) once told me, "The best engineers sometimes come in bodies that can't talk," and Bushnell emphasized that to hire—and get the most from—the best engineers, you have to look at what they do rather than say. When a knowledgeable person isn't saying much, a boss's job is to ask "what do you think?"

Understand the Work You Manage—Or Get Out of the Way

Walt Disney of the Walt Disney Company, Bill Gates at Microsoft, Larry Ellison of Oracle, Steve Jobs of Apple, Ed Catmull at Pixar, Ray Kroc of McDonald's, Anne Mulcahy at Xerox, Marissa Mayer of Google, Hasso Plattner of SAP, and George Zimmer of the Men's Wearhouse were (and in some cases still are) financially successful bosses. They made their marks in diverse industries, and their personalities varied wildly; yet they are similar in that each had a deep understanding of the work they led.

After Kroc bought the franchise rights from the McDonald brothers, he ran the first McDonald's restaurant outside of California, in Des Plaines, Illinois. Even though he was CEO of the growing chain, Kroc devoted obsessive attention to the operation and did every job from cooking to cleaning bathrooms. Fred Turner, who became McDonald's head of operations, reported: "Every night, you would see him coming down the street, walking close to the gutter, picking up every McDonald's wrapper and cup along the way. He'd come into the store with his hands full of cups and wrappers. He was the store's outside pick-up man." Years later, when Kroc visited other franchises, he would first walk around the parking lot and pick up the trash. Then he went in to talk about maintaining QSC: quality, service, and cleanliness. The QSC system was developed by Fred Turner—who knew the work, too, as he started out grilling hamburgers at Kroc's Des Plaines store.

You don't have to be a founder or CEO to understand the work. Last year, I was given a tour of the Operations Control Center for the Bay Area Rapid Transit (BART), a train system that serves much of the San Francisco area. My guide was BART's chief transportation officer, Rudy Crespo, who had worked at BART for over thirty years. Rudy explained to me how people in the nerve center coordinated their work with field employees. Their jobs included managing train movement, scheduling, communications, security, power management, emergency response, and a supervisor in charge of the operation who reported to Rudy. I asked Rudy how many of those jobs he had done: He replied, "All of them." Rudy was impossible to fool with smart talk. And when something went wrong, his people told me that Rudy just about always knew the fastest way to fix it.

In an ideal world, bosses would always manage work they understood deeply. But it isn't always feasible. Every boss can't have deep knowledge of every follower's expertise. When that happens, a boss's job is to ask good questions, listen, defer to those with greater expertise, and, above all, to accept his or her own ignorance. Those who fail to do so risk making bad decisions and ruining their reputations. In Gerald Weinberg's classic *The Psychology of Computer Programming*, he provides a cautionary tale about "Arnold," a salesperson put in charge of a group of programmers. Rather than deferring to their knowledge, Arnold insisted that he knew an algorithm that would solve the team's most pressing problem. He showed it to two experienced programmers. Rather than telling their boss that it was wrong, they encouraged him to present it to the whole team. Then, "they gave him about five minutes to get himself solidly enmeshed in his own snare. Then they began to tear his algorithm apart—in detail as well as in grand plan." Arnold was laughed out of the room and soon transferred to another job.

In contrast, Bill George demonstrated the power of listening and learning when he took charge of a company with work practices and technologies he did not understand. Bill led Medtronic as it grew from a medical device company valued at 1 billion dollars in 1989 to 60 billion dollars in 2002. Bill told me that he was new to the industry when he joined Medtronic, so during his first nine months he spent over half of his time in hospitals, watching surgical teams install Medtronic devices and talking to them as well as patients, families, and administrators. Even after that, Bill was careful to defer to the expertise of surgeons, nurses, and hospital administrators. But he felt better equipped to understand their concerns and to ask them useful questions.

Empathy for Customers

The Bill George story illustrates that to understand the work, a boss needs to develop both technical knowledge and empathy. Yet, although every boss knows better, it amazes me how ignorant many are about what it feels like to be one of their customers. In my opinion, one reason that General Motors got into such a mind-boggling mess (they declared bankruptcy in 2009 and survived only because of a massive government bailout) is that bosses throughout the company were oblivious to the experience of owning a GM car. For years, GM had a perk for managers and other white-collar workers (down to fairly low levels) where they were given a free GM car to drive. A retired GM manager told me that senior executives got more expensive cars than less-senior employees eligible for the program. But so long as those guidelines were followed, he explained, "employees could order any car they wanted. We had a full-time office staff and a room where you went to spec out and order your car. There was no cost to the employee, insurance was free, and you filled up at a pump next to the building. Execs, I think, had some way to signal they needed gas and someone would fill it for them."

So not only were thousands of the most powerful people at GM insulated from the typically dreadful experience of selecting a car, haggling over the price, dealing with the financing, and trading in an old car—they were spared the hassle of visiting a gas station and forking out their own money for fuel.

Conversations with current and former GM employees plus a *Detroit News* story indicate that a version of this program still exists. It works something like this: The lowest-level GM managers and other white-collar workers have to buy their own cars; the ones at somewhat higher levels get a new car every six months or so but have to arrange their own servicing; higher-ranking executives get fancier cars and are relieved from dealing with much of the servicing. Executives at the very top of the heap get a car and a driver—and thus are perfectly protected from any aspect of selecting, buying, servicing, selling, or driving a car. Over the years, the program has evolved from a free benefit to one costing employees $150 a month to one costing $250 a month (as of October, 2008)—still a darn good deal for a new car every 6 months, maintenance, insurance, and gasoline.

A few years before the shit really hit the fan at GM (when the cost was still $150 a month), I made a forceful—well, downright obnoxious—complaint to some GM managers about this program: I argued it should be abolished immediately because it blinded managers and executives to many parts of the car ownership experience. They answered that GM couldn't possibly get rid of the program because they had negotiated a great tax deal with the state of Michigan (much better than Ford, they bragged) and it was one of the few perks left for white-collar employees. To be fair, these managers pointed out they did go to dealerships to buy cars for family members. I reminded them, however, that this experience was still misleading as they were given a preset (and very low) GM price—sparing them from the unpleasant and sometimes combative process of haggling over the price. I was not very nice; I argued that this mentality was one reason the company was in trouble and would get in more trouble. They treated me like I was insane.

When bosses make concerted efforts to understand what it feels like to be a customer, it makes gaps between knowledge and action vivid and helps them identify more effective repairs. To illustrate, SYPartners (SYP), an innovation firm based in San Francisco and New York, worked with up-and-coming executives from a big company to develop new financial services for immigrants. The executives arrived with armloads of binders packed with data-rich PowerPoint decks—and they were excited about how well they had mastered the charts and statistics. They got nervous when SYP told them they weren't going to use that stuff and instead would be shadowing customers.

SYP broke the team into trios, assigned each a Spanish-speaking translator and a Spanish-speaking undocumented worker, and sent them out to the Mission District in San Francisco. Each team was asked to cash a check in a bank, wire money to a Central American country at Western Union, and observe the undocumented worker do the same things. Before the observations, these executives knew from their quantitative data that these untapped customers represented a huge opportunity. But their impressions of what these customers wanted—and would happily pay for—were far off the mark. The shadowing, hands-on efforts, and discussions with undocumented workers provoked them to transform and broaden the offerings they suggested to their firm. One executive called it "life-changing" and said he would never look at a marketing opportunity the same again. The executive who initially felt most uncomfortable about following around an illegal immigrant came away most transformed—arguing adamantly that reams of data aren't enough, that you need to understand what your customers do and how it feels to be them.

Be Repetitive and Concrete

Think of "the Miracle on the Hudson," the crippled Airbus A320 that made a water landing in New York in January 2009. Captain Chesley B. "Sully" Sullenberg III deserves massive credit for the feat. But the "miracle" was also a testament to the veteran flight attendants. As Flight 1549 plummeted down, they chanted in unison to passengers, "Brace, brace, heads down, stay down," preventing many injuries during the rough landing. Repetitive and concrete guidance isn't just effective during emergencies. It is something that bosses who want their words to provoke action learn to do. To bring together the notions of simplicity and repetition, former Procter & Gamble executive Claudia Kotchka heard A. G. Lafley repeat his *"Sesame Street Simple"* mantra many times to many different people during his decade as P&G's CEO. Claudia told me that she was always struck by how strongly most people were stirred when they heard A. G. say it for the first time—or even the third or fourth.

The things you say over and over have the most impact if they specify what to do and when to do it. As a boss, your job is to find the equivalent of "Brace, brace, heads down, stay down" for your followers. The power of concreteness is seen in an experiment reported by Lee Ross and Richard Nisbett. A group of Stanford students were asked to think of their peers and pick both the generous soul most likely to contribute to a food drive and the selfish jerk least likely to donate. The researchers then contacted the "generous" and "jerk" peers and asked them to contribute to a food drive. They split the peers into two groups. One group got vague directions, just a letter addressed "Dear Student" that asked them to donate food and told them where to do it. The other students were addressed by name in the letter, given directions about what food to donate (e.g., a can of beans), a map showing where the drop box was, a specific time to donate it, and a follow-up call to remind them what, when, and where to donate. When the directions were vague, 8 percent of the generous students donated food, but not one of the jerks did so. Concreteness packed a big wallop: 25 percent of the jerks donated food when they were given specific guidance; well behind the 43 percent of generous students given concrete directions, but far better than none at all.

Checklists create especially strong connective tissue between words and concrete deeds. The pre-takeoff checklists that pilots use were developed before World War II. The Army's chief of flight testing, Major Ployer Hill, made an easily avoidable mistake in 1935 and crashed a prototype B-17 bomber. Critics complained it was impossible to fly the B-17 safely because doing so required so many steps—which nearly drove Boeing into bankruptcy. The solution was a checklist "with step-by-step checks for takeoff, flight, landing, and taxiing," which helped thousands of pilots fly B-17s safely for millions of miles. Recent research also suggests that when doctors and nurses use simple checklists with patients who have intravenous lines in their veins, infections and deaths drop dramatically. After checklists were instituted in one hospital, the infection rate dropped from 11 percent to 0 percent.

Keep It Simple, Stupid

These examples of repetitive and concrete talk all employ simple language. Yet getting people to use simple language isn't always easy. Smart talkers have considerable incentive for saying things that are incomprehensible. Unfortunately, people who spew out incomprehensible "jargon monoxide"* are rated as smarter than those who use simple words—especially when they are renowned for their expertise. This attribution even occurs when people use unintelligible language to mask meaningless and useless ideas. So beware that when people seem so smart that you can't understand a word they say, these pretenders may have learned that blasting out jargon monoxide is the best way to get ahead and mask their incompetence at the same time.

Authentic experts have no incompetence to mask but must beware of "the curse of knowledge": The more people know about something, the harder it is for them to package explanations and instructions in ways that others can comprehend. Stanford's Pamela Hinds, for example, showed that people with the greatest expertise at operating a cell phone did the worst job of teaching novices to

---

* I thank Polly LaBarre for introducing me to this phrase.

operate the phone. This curse happens because experts have a hard time putting themselves in the shoes of neophytes. Experts' actions become so automatic to them that they forget the simple steps they had to learn and other struggles they faced as novices. Some experts also resist dumbing things down because they are so impressed with their own brilliance—and so disdainful of those who lack it—that they view people who can't understand them as dolts. I once saw an R&D manager teach a supply-chain workshop that the audience couldn't follow because it was packed with convoluted statistics, incomprehensible graphs, and obscure jargon. After the workshop, he muttered to me, "I guess this is where we keep the people who aren't the sharpest tools in the shed." He had no clue that few people on the planet had the expertise required to understand his strange language and complex arguments.

The best bosses battle unnecessary intricacy, serving as simplicity police who relentlessly reduce the emotional and cognitive effort required for turning knowledge into action. The saying "Keep It Simple, Stupid," or the KISS philosophy, has been applied by bosses from Colonel Harland Sanders (founder of Kentucky Fried Chicken) to Procter & Gamble to animation director Richard Williams, who is most famous for *Who Framed Roger Rabbit*. KISS sounds silly, but it works. As we've seen, no matter how much you know, influencing others' actions is impossible unless you can translate your brilliance into steps that human beings can grasp and apply.

Chip and Dan Heath teach us that if you want a simple and concrete message to pack the biggest wallop, package it in a story that people will remember and spread. Consider what allegedly happened when Conrad Hilton (founder of the Hilton Hotel chain) appeared on Johnny Carson's NBC *Tonight Show* in the 1960s: Johnny asked him if there was anything he wanted to say to the millions of people in the TV audience. Hilton looked into the camera and said: "Yes, please remember to put the shower curtain *inside* the tub." I am not entirely sure if this is a true story, and if it is true, Hilton may have said it elsewhere: Some claim Hilton said it on his deathbed. True or not, it is a perfect model for a story that people remember and that shapes behavior—it is simple, concrete, and specifies precisely what actions to take. I think of Conrad Hilton every time I stay in a hotel that has shower curtains. As I put the curtain inside the tub, I hear the story in my head every time—and I can see Johnny Carson laughing at the story in my mind's eye, even though I never actually saw it happen.

Simple Metrics

This quest for simplicity also means using clear and actionable metrics—and as few as possible. As Jeff Pfeffer and I showed in *The Knowing-Doing Gap*, too many organizations suffer from what we call the Otis Redding Problem. We wrote, "Recall the line from his old song 'Sitting on the Dock of the Bay': 'Can't do what ten people tell me to do, so I guess I'll remain the same.' That's the problem with holding people, groups, or businesses to too many metrics: They can't satisfy or even think about all of them at once, so they end up doing what they want or the one or two things they believe are important or that will bring them rewards (regardless of senior management's strategic intent)." In the years since we described the Otis Redding Problem, I've encountered hundreds of people who are judged by absurdly long lists of metrics, from the Microsoft vice president who explained that it was hard for him to remember all thirty-five measures on his "scorecard" to the Intuit supply-chain manager who proudly announced (along with the consultant who helped him do it) to a large audience that he had just implemented Intuit's one hundredth supply-chain metric.

Yet it is possible to battle the Otis Redding Problem, to employ a few key metrics so people know where to devote their efforts. This is what COO Joe Mello did at DaVita, which operates over 1,200 kidney dialysis centers in the United States. DaVita employs about 30,000 people and serves over 100,000 patients. When Joe discovered that part of his company suffered from the Otis Redding Problem, he did something about it. As Joe wrote us:

A few months ago I took over the oversight for our revenue operations (billing and collections). In the new combined company we have about 900 FTEs (Full-Time

Equivalents) in this area and we had just hired a great senior executive to run it. It is really complicated. It was (and still is) a mess....We went from 42 really important measures to 9 reeeaaallllyyy important ones. And progress has begun!

Joe's spirit captures the essence of a great boss. Once he discovered an impediment to action, he didn't just talk about it—he removed it.

Simple Strategies

Another misguided trick bosses use to demonstrate their brilliance—at least to themselves—is to develop incomprehensible strategies. Unfortunately, if your people can't understand your strategy, they can't figure out what to do. And, even if they can comprehend the twists and turns, the complexity can scatter their attention in so many directions that they won't do any single thing well. One of the most striking transformations I've ever seen from a convoluted strategy to a simple one was done by Steve Jobs. When Jobs took over Apple in July 1997, the company sold a dizzying array of computers—at least twenty different kinds. Jobs had been banished from Apple for a decade. So he spent his first few weeks back on the job trying to figure out what was going on, which included trying to grasp Apple's product strategy. He asked insiders to explain the differences among products like the Performa 3400, 4400, 5400, and 6500. He discovered: "I couldn't figure it out. We couldn't even tell our friends which ones to buy." This strategy confused customers, made it hard to figure out where to focus product development and marketing efforts, and mucked up the company's supply chain. Within a year, Jobs had discontinued all these products, leaving Apple with just four computers to sell: a business laptop and desktop, and a consumer laptop and desktop. So began Apple's return to profitability and reemergence as a great company, which cemented Job's reputation as a ruthless genius.

Do It and You Will Know

Taking action and seeing what you can get done (and learn) as you muddle forward is among the most effective antidotes to the smart-talk trap. I am not saying that talking, brainstorming, and doing research are a waste of time; they're all extremely useful—but only when used as stepping stones to action, not as ends themselves. Debra Dunn, Kris Woyzbun, and I apply this perspective in our Stanford class "Treating Organizational Practices as Prototypes." Our students have implemented prototypes to reduce stress and boredom for passengers on delayed flights, provide timely performance feedback at software firms, and improve the employee orientation process at a consulting firm.

My favorite prototype was developed for Timbuk2, a San Francisco company that makes trendy carrying bags and related accessories. The CEO at the time (in 2008) was the straight talking Perry Klebahn: He told us they had a terrible all-hands meeting and wondered if our students had ideas about fixing it. We brought the entire class (twelve students) to Timbuk2 to observe the meeting, which was attended by about seventy employees. Perry was right—it was awful: we couldn't tell who was in charge; there was no agenda, no discussion of products or customers; most people stood uncomfortably; new employees were not introduced; there was no food or drink; the late afternoon sun glared through the windows (making it hot and uncomfortable); everyone looked bored and one employee fell asleep.

After the meeting, our students listed problems and brainstormed solutions. The next week, when four managers (including Perry) from Timbuk2 visited us, the students first had us all role-play the current meeting. We stood up in a disorganized mess, with no agenda and no enthusiasm, and, of course, a student pretended to be asleep. After a few minutes, they made a dramatic shift, and we role-played a new and improved meeting: Chairs and food were rolled in, someone took charge, newcomers were introduced and each told a little personal story, a customer talked about the pluses and minuses of Timbuk2 products, along with many other changes. Leaders at Timbuk2 began implementing many of these ideas immediately, and our interviews—even with the company's most cynical employees—revealed the meeting was much improved. This change from a rotten meeting to a pretty good one took only about two weeks—largely because the students' observations, brainstorming, and role-playing were so tightly linked to tangible actions. Timbuk2's leaders didn't just thank the students for their ideas: They tried (and refined) them so they would know if they worked. These bosses demonstrated, as Walt Disney is believed to have said, "the way to get started is to quit talking and begin doing."

Do What Is Right, Not What Everyone Else Does

Mindless imitation is among the most dangerous and widespread forms of management idiocy. One of the dumbest excuses for screwing up is "everyone else does it, it is industry standard." It reminds me of something that one of my college friends liked to say: "Eat shit. Ten billion flies can't be wrong." But being a copycat is also one of the safest excuses. When everyone else does nothing at all, or all do the same inane thing, such collective stupidity makes people feel far better than when they do the same, equally moronic things on their own.

This is exactly the excuse offered by the many bankers and mortgage brokers who gave loans to people for houses they couldn't afford in the run-up to the 2008 financial meltdown—even though many now say that they knew it was wrong at the time. Keysha Cooper was a mortgage underwriter at the now-defunct Washington Mutual. Ms. Cooper reported, "They didn't care if we were giving loans to people that didn't qualify. Instead, it was how many loans did you guys close and fund?" Ms. Cooper's superiors repeatedly scolded her and placed negative written reports in her personnel file because she turned down bad loans. We now know this was reckless and stupid, but WaMu was following "industry standard" at the time. My mother taught me to think for myself when trying to decide what to do—which was good advice when I was a teenager, because many of my friends were idiots. It is good advice for bosses, too. Don't mindlessly compare yourself to others. What is right for them could be wrong for you. Worse yet, the people you imitate might be complete dolts.

Hot Emotions and Cool Solutions

Bosses who avoid the smart-talk trap make it essential (and easy) for people to link what they know to what they do. Check out the "Stepping Stones for Can-Do Bosses," which recaps many of the tips and tricks here for closing knowing-doing gaps. A topic that I've only touched on lightly, however, is the challenge of charging up people to take action. As we've seen, dispensing rewards for smart actions and creating psychological safety are part of the answer. But if you really want to fuel intense action, the one-two punch of, *first*, creating "hot" emotions about some problem, challenge, or enemy and, *second*, steering all that passion to "cool," or rational, solutions is the recipe for success.

Evidence for the power of linking hot emotions to cool solutions comes from research by my Stanford colleague Hayagreeva "Huggy" Rao. For example, Huggy describes how, when Fritz Maytag bought a struggling San Francisco brewery called Anchor Steam in 1965, his intention was to spend a few years turning around the place, then sell it. But he quickly became enamored with brewing and emerged as a leader in the "Battle of Beers." Fritz mobilized excitement and support among his employees, customers, home brewers, and other craft brewers against "industrial beers" like Coors and Corona, which he called "thin, tasteless, watery, and over-carbonated, a source of inebriation rather than taste."

Fritz, who has now owned Anchor Steam for forty-five years, has devoted himself to working with employees and fellow craft brewers to develop methods for producing better and more consistent beers. From the beginning, he has encouraged and advised newcomers to the microbrewing business so they can make good beer and market and distribute it effectively—treating them as allies in a battle against a common enemy rather than as competitors. Fritz has helped turn talk into action by first stirring hot emotions about the enemy, those "bland" and "sticky-sweet" industrial beers. Second, Fritz has served as a visible and persistent force behind the development of diverse rational solutions (e.g., production, marketing, and distribution techniques) that have enabled Anchor Steam and hundreds of other microbreweries and brew pubs to grab a modest, but respectable, share of the beer market. The beers produced by Anchor Steam now yield about 5 million dollars a year in revenue and are sold in all fifty states.

As Fritz Maytag's story shows, if you want to incite action among your people—or a network of partners or customers—start by cranking up the emotion: Get people angry by naming the enemy, or get them excited by identifying compelling dreams and goals. Then find ways to harness and aim all that energy to provide tangible and effective bridges between knowledge and action.

STEPPING STONES FOR CAN-DO BOSSES

Tips and Tricks for Eradicating Impediments to Action

1. **When your people suggest a promising idea, say (as often as possible): "Great! Do it!"** This is inspired by a UPS commercial, where two slick consultants propose cost-cutting ideas to a receptive client. He replies: "Great! Do it!" The consultants look bewildered and respond, "Sir, we don't actually do what we propose. We just propose it." In contrast, the best bosses and followers do what they propose.

2. **Assign your worst smart talkers to shadow your best doers.** Reward *both* parties if the smart talkers become more action oriented.

3. **Fire or demote incurable smart talkers—and let your people know why you did it.** Beware of creating

a climate of fear, so give people feedback and warnings first. But if you let these rotten apples stick around, they will infect others and produce vile consequences for all.

4. **Say the same simple and good things again and again until the message shapes what people do.** You might start by borrowing the "*Sesame Street* Simple" philosophy from A. G. Lafley.

5. **Tell juicy stories about destructive things to stop doing—and simple things to start.** One manager often tells a story about his past bad behavior on conference calls. When he wasn't talking, he tuned out the conversation and answered e-mails. He kept missing important things (like the time a key employee quit), and his direct reports concluded such detachment meant he didn't care about them or their work. Now he turns off his monitor during calls and imagines his people are in the room.

6. **When in doubt, throw it out or don't add it in the first place.** Follow Steve Jobs and try to explain to one another—and customers—the differences among your products and services. If you can't do so easily, perhaps it is time to get rid of a bunch.

7. **Fight the Otis Redding Problem.** List all the performance metrics you use. No matter how long it is, pick the three most important. Do you really need the rest?

8. **Ask yourself—and your people—if you have practices that "everyone else" uses, but are a waste of time or downright destructive.** What about your performance evaluations? People who give and receive them usually hate the process. They are usually done so badly that they do more harm than good. Would you be better off not doing them at

all—or at least cutting 75 percent of the questions on your form?

9. **Link hot emotions to cool actions.** Crank up your people's fears and hopes to get their juices flowing, then direct that energy to effective and concrete behaviors. Like the financial services executives who kept talking about the need to get more young customers. They got really worked up about it when they recruited twenty-something customers to try their services, which resulted in horror stories about insensitive employees and incomprehensible marketing materials. The executives were then properly inspired to develop practices to chip away at the problem.

Chapter 6

Serve as a Human Shield

The best bosses let the workers do their work. They protect their people from red tape, meddlesome executives, nosy visitors, unnecessary meetings, and a host of other insults, intrusions and time wasters. The notion that management "buffers" the core work of the organization from uncertainty and external perturbations is an old theme in organization theory. A good boss takes pride in serving as a human shield, absorbing and deflecting heat from superiors and customers, doing all manner of boring and silly tasks, and battling back against every idiot and slight that makes life unfair or harder than necessary on his or her charges.

The main test here is whether or not followers believe their boss has got their backs. Robert Townsend could have been the poster child for the boss as a human shield. As I mentioned earlier, Townsend held a host of management jobs including CEO of Avis Rent-a-Car and wrote the inspired and outrageous *Up the Organization*. In Townsend's mind, a boss's job was to "work for your people," which meant being a defender and warrior on their behalf. He once refused to provide an Avis board member, David Sarnoff, with a complete tally of all the cars that Avis owned. Weeks of work would be required to assemble such information; Townsend believed his people's efforts were better spent elsewhere. So he shot back at Sarnoff: "If I don't need it to run the company, you sure as hell don't need that information as an outside director." Earlier in Townsend's career at American Express, the firm's chairman stopped him in the hall to praise a "good bond swap" by his group. Townsend replied that he didn't know about it, because he was devoting all his time to scrounging for resources and better pay for the undervalued "peons" doing this magnificent work. Townsend used the encounter with his superior to fight for his people, not to bask in the reflected glory of their accomplishments.

Along similar lines, I interviewed Captain Nick Gottuso, of the Hillsborough, California, police department, to discover how he helps protect his officers' backs. Nick emphasized that he not only shields them from unnecessary intrusions and hassles, he also strives to protect their emotional well-being. In addition to his regular job, Nick serves as one of the commanders of a SWAT team staffed by about fifty officers from local police departments. SWAT teams are called in for risky operations like serving warrants to dangerous suspects, dealing with barricaded suspects, rescuing hostages, and other crises beyond the capabilities of regular police officers.

Nick described an ugly hostage situation that unfolded in San Mateo, California, on November 25, 2008. An armed intruder, twenty-two-year-old Raymond Gee, entered a family's home and threatened twenty-four-year-old Loan Kim Nguyen and her two children. Within forty-five minutes, forty or so SWAT team members had the house surrounded. Nguyen managed to barricade herself and her children in a bedroom, then lowered her two children onto the roof of the SWAT truck from a second-story window. But just as the second child was lowered to safety, the intruder fired ten rounds through a wall from the next room and fatally shot her. The SWAT team fired dozens of rounds in an attempt to kill the intruder (and now murderer), who was later found dead, killed by his own hand.

After the incident ended, Nick knew his officers were upset because they couldn't save Loan Kim Nguyen and were worried because they had fired their weapons. (Officers learn that doing so can get them in legal and political trouble, even when it was clearly the right thing to do.) Nick told me, "I walked up to each of the officers on my team who had fired their weapons, looked each one in the eye, patted them on the back or gave them a hug, and said, 'You did a great job, I am damn proud of you.'" Nick explained that such reassurance and affection helped his officers deal with the emotions of the moment and eased their worries that if legal or political issues did arise, he was in their corner and would fight for them with all his might.

Whether a boss has an office job like Robert Townsend

or works under extreme conditions like Nick Gottuso, a big part of the job is shielding followers from unnecessary and destructive worries, hassles, procedures, indignities, and intruders and idiots of every stripe.

Don't Waste Their Time

If you are determined to be an effective shield, start by working on yourself. Great bosses avoid burdening their people. They invent, borrow, and implement ways to reduce the mental and emotional load they heap on followers. In particular, meetings are notorious time and energy suckers. Yes, some are necessary, but too many bosses run them in ways that disrespect people's time and dignity—especially self-absorbed bosses bent on self-glorification. If you want to grab power and don't care much about your people, make sure you arrive a little late to most meetings. Plus, every now and then, show up *very* late, or—better yet—send word after everyone has gathered that, alas, you must cancel the meeting because something more pressing has come up. After all, if you are a *very important person*, the little people need to accept their inferior social standing.

Sound familiar? Using arrival times to display and grab power is an ancient trick. This move was used by elders, or "Big Men," in primitive tribes to gain and reinforce status. An ethnography of the Merina tribe in Madagascar found that jostling for status among elders meant that gatherings routinely started three or four hours late. Elders used young boys to spy on each other and played a waiting game that dragged on for hours. Each elder worked to maximize the impression that the moment he arrived, the meeting started. If he arrived early and the meeting didn't start right away, it signaled that he wasn't the alpha male. If he arrived late and the meeting had started without him, it also signaled that he wasn't the most prestigious elder. I've seen similar power plays in academia. I was once on a committee led by a prestigious faculty member who always arrived at least ten minutes late, often twenty minutes. He also cancelled two meetings after the rest of the five-person committee had gathered. I tracked the time I wasted waiting for this jerk, which totaled over a half day during a six-month stretch.

A related move is to insist that people stay beyond the scheduled ending time, making them late for other meetings or friends and families. Sure, sometimes staying late is necessary because of a pressing deadline. But a smart organizational politician knows this move is a way to grab power, too. Keeping people late demonstrates that you aren't just more important than everyone else in the room: The ripple effects on other meetings, family dinners, and so on show you are more important than everyone else in their lives, too. In contrast, if you want your people to have more time to do work, be treated with dignity, and be proud to work for you, then start and end meetings on time. You might miss the thrill of petty power displays, but perhaps you can glean some prestige from having productive and grateful followers.

Along related lines, don't feel compelled to use all the scheduled meeting time if you can wrap up early. My past dean in the Stanford Engineering School, John Hennessy, was the master of this and other "don't dither" methods. In most meetings, we would discuss each item briefly and then John would answer decisively: yes, no, or "I can't tell you now; I need more information." Most meetings took about half the scheduled time. I was shocked after the first one (after all, most academics act as if time has no value), but I soon appreciated how John showed respect for others' time and left time for his other chores. John's skills were noticed by many at Stanford, as he rose from dean, to provost, to president in just a few years.

Will Wright, designer of computer games, including The Sims and Spore, used an employee-centered method for keeping meetings short. Wright invited artist Ocean Quigley to meetings because he was so creative and so impatient. He treated Quigley "like the canary in the coal mine." When Quigley raised his hand and asked to be excused, "that was the point we knew that the meeting had hit diminishing returns" and it was time to end it.

There are sometimes even better reasons to end early. Declaring defeat before the scheduled ending provides an escape from useless, boring, or destructive meetings. Doing so is far better than prolonging the misery or allowing the damage to keep piling up. I used this tactic a few years back when coaching a girls' soccer team. We had a guest at one practice, an experienced player from England to teach skills that were beyond the three of us dads who coached the girls. We had been helped by these English coaches before, and they had been charming and remarkably helpful. The coach that day was a nightmare. He was impatient and acted angry and depressed. He mumbled so quietly and had such a thick Cockney accent that we couldn't understand him. One girl after another asked me, "Why is he so mad at us?" and "What is he saying?" Practice was scheduled to run an hour, but after enduring this grumpy Brit for forty minutes, I declared practice over and sent everyone home.

Finally, rather than automatically scheduling a meeting, ask yourself if you really need it or doing so is just a knee-jerk reaction. Will Wright used a nice little trick. Every time someone called a meeting, he charged them a dollar. Although Will went to a lot of meetings and got a lot of dollars, "It did make them think twice, even though it was only a dollar."

In Praise of Stand-Up Meetings

I've been fascinated by stand-up meetings for years. It started when Jeff Pfeffer and I were writing *Hard Facts, Dangerous Half-Truths, and Total Nonsense,* our book on evidence-based management. We often met in Jeff's lovely house, typically starting out in his kitchen. But we usually ended up in Jeff's spacious study—where we both stood— or, more often, Jeff sat on the lone chair and I stood. Meetings in his study were productive but rarely lasted long.

There was no place for me to sit, and the discomfort soon drove me out the door (or at least back to the kitchen). We wondered if there was research on stand-up meetings, and to our delight, we found an experiment comparing decisions made by fifty-six groups where people stood up during meetings to fifty-five groups where people sat down. These were short meetings, in the ten- to twenty-minute range, but the researchers found big differences. Groups that stood up took 34 percent less time to make the assigned decision, and there were no significant differences in decision quality between stand-up and sit-down groups.

Stand-up meetings aren't just praised in cute academic studies. Robert Townsend advised in *Up the Organization*, "Some meetings should be mercifully brief. A good way to handle the latter is to hold the meeting with everyone standing up. The meetees won't believe you at first. Then they get very uncomfortable and can hardly wait to get the meeting over with."

I keep finding good bosses who use stand-up meetings to speed things along. One is David Darragh, CEO of Reily, a New Orleans–based company that specializes in Southern foods and drinks. They produce and market dozens of products such as Wick Fowler's 2-Alarm Chili, CDM Coffee and Chicory, No Pudge Fat Free Brownie Mix, and Luzianne Tea. David and I were having a rollicking conversation about how he works with his team. I started interrogating closely after he mentioned the fifteen-minute stand-up meeting held in his office four mornings a week. We since exchanged a series of e-mails about these meetings. As David explains:

> The importance of the stand-up meeting is that it can be accomplished efficiently and, therefore, with greater frequency. Like many areas of discipline, repetition begets improved results. The same is true with meetings. The rhythm that frequency generates allows relationships to develop, personal ticks to be understood, stressors to be identified, personal strengths and weaknesses to be put out in the light of day, etc. The role of stand-up meetings is not to work on strategic issues or even to resolve an immediate issue. The role is to bubble up the issues of the day and to identify the ones that need to be worked on outside the meeting and agree on a steward to be responsible for it. With frequent, crisp stand-up meetings, there can never be the excuse that the opportunity to communicate was not there. We insist that bad news travels just as fast as good news.

The team also has a ninety-minute sit-down meeting each week, where they dig into more strategic issues. But the quick daily meetings keep the team connected, allow them to spot small problems before they become big ones, and facilitate quick and effective action.

Stand-up meetings aren't right for every meeting or boss. As we saw in the last chapter in the broken Timbuk2 all-hands meeting, part of the problem with that forty-five-minute gathering was there was no place for most people to sit, which fueled the group's grumpiness and impatience. The key lesson is that the best bosses keep hunting for little ways to use everyone's time and energy more efficiently and respectfully. They keep unearthing traditions, procedures, or other things that needlessly slow people down. In many cases, these speed bumps have been around so long that people don't even realize they exist or do more harm than good. Try to look at what you and your people do through fresh eyes. Bring in someone who doesn't know any better and ask them: What can I do to help my people travel through the day with fewer hassles?

External Time Suckers

Henry Mintzberg's path-breaking research on managerial work showed that a good boss doggedly protects followers from outsiders. He wrote, "Someone once defined a manager, half in jest, as someone who sees the visitors so that everyone else can get the work done." If you are a boss, protecting yourself from intrusions may be a lost cause. Mintzberg showed that doing management work requires dozens—sometimes hundreds—of brief and fragmented tasks each day. A study of manufacturing foremen found that they dealt with an average of 583 "incidents," or little chunks of work, each day—with a range of 237 to 1,037 incidents. And this was before e-mail was invented. Work is more fragmented now because, for most bosses (and everyone else), e-mails and instant messages mean we are bombarded with important—and more often enticing but trivial—interruptions from anywhere in the world at any time.

You may not have to deal with over five hundred incidents a day like those foremen did, but a hallmark of managerial work is that—whether you are a CEO or a supervisor—it entails one interruption after another. A skilled boss shields his or her people by intercepting and dealing with many messages, problems, people, and assignments, so his or her people can focus on their work. Interruptions are especially destructive to people who need to concentrate—knowledge workers like hardware engineers, graphic designers, lawyers, writers, architects, accountants, and so on. Research by Gloria Mark and her colleagues shows that it takes people an average of twenty-five minutes to recover from an interruption and return to the task they had been working on—which happens because interruptions destroy their train of thought and divert attention to other tasks. A related study shows that although employees who experience interruptions compensate by working faster when they return to what they were doing, this speed comes at a cost, including feeling frustrated, stressed, and harried. Some interruptions are unavoidable and are part of the work—but as a boss, the more trivial and unnecessary intrusions you can absorb, the more work your people will do and the less their mental health will suffer.

Bosses also protect their people's time by buffering

them from organizational practices that are annoying and excessively burdensome. Rather than accepting practices sent from above as unchangeable, proactive bosses redesign them. Consider Bonny Warner-Simi, the JetBlue pilot and executive that I quoted in chapter 3. Bonny is one of the most proactive and effective bosses I know. She formed her can-do attitude as a member of three U.S. Winter Olympics teams, where she competed in the luge, and during her years working as a commercial airline pilot between the Olympics.

In 2007, Bonny and her management team felt burdened by JetBlue's performance evaluation process. The form took about two hours to complete and required much frustrating back-and-forth between boss and employee. They scrapped the old form and designed one that took only twenty minutes to complete. The new form is clearer and still quite comprehensive, covering fourteen competencies, four performance goals, and one trajectory. And it is closely linked to JetBlue's strategy. This shorter form not only lightens the load on bosses and employees (with no apparent loss of crucial information), it frees time that Bonny and her direct reports now use to prepare for and speed along meetings in which they discuss their subordinates' performance. Bonny explained, "The magic part is the simple form, but then we also run a calibration of the trajectories (underperforming, well placed, expanded role, or promotable). Each director presents a two- to three-minute speech on the reasons why they feel their managers are on a specific trajectory. Then there is debate and discussion. That way, we get a much richer perspective on performance and can ensure that managers are rated fairly across disciplines."

Ignore and Defy Idiocy from on High

Bonny Warner-Simi and her team reinvented their evaluation form with the support and permission of senior executives. JetBlue executives knew there were problems with the system and were glad that Bonny's group was trying something new. Too often, however, senior leaders or powerful staff groups cram their crummy ideas down people's throats. Unfortunately, sometimes the best thing for your people—and your career—is to cave in to these silly demands and do as you are told. The political costs of defying superiors or a powerful group might be just too great. Wise bosses also remind themselves and their people that orders and procedures imposed from on high that—at first blush—seem idiotic occasionally actually turn out to be useful and necessary. Good bosses dig into the facts, and if possible, follow the fate of fellow bosses who have implemented the apparently crummy ideas before deciding whether to adopt or resist a new directive.

The best bosses find the sweet spot between acting like spineless wimps who always do just as they are told (no matter how absurd) versus insubordinate rabble-rousers who challenge and ignore every order and standard operating procedure. Good bosses try to cooperate with superiors and do what is best for their organizations, but they realize that defiance can be required to protect their people and themselves—and sometimes is even ultimately appreciated by superiors. 3M CEO William McKnight repeatedly threatened to fire Richard Drew back in the 1920s because he was fiddling with a pet project rather than devoting 100 percent of his time to his quality-control job. McKnight realized he was wrong when that pet project turned out to be masking tape, which soon became the most successful product in the company's history. McKnight apologized to Drew and instituted the now-famous 15 percent rule, where employees are encouraged to spend 15 percent of their time on any pet project they want.

Similarly, Chuck House was leading a development team at Hewlett-Packard in the late 1960s when CEO David Packard ordered them to stop working on it, as he believed that the oscilloscope they were designing wouldn't interest customers. Chuck said, "Yes, boss," but he really didn't mean it. Instead, Chuck spent his vacation getting several million dollars' worth of orders for the machine. Packard not only let Chuck's team build it, but a few years later Packard led a ceremony where he awarded House a medal for "extraordinary contempt and defiance beyond the normal call of engineering duty."

Robert Townsend would have applauded Chuck's defiance. He wrote of "disobedience and its necessity" and encouraged bosses to follow Napoleon's advice: "[A]ny commander-in-chief who undertakes to carry out a plan which he considers to be defective is at fault; he must put forward his reasons, insist on the plan being changed, and finally tender his resignation rather than be the instrument of his army's downfall."

Sometimes, however, a boss can avoid open disobedience by simply ignoring a superior's idiocy and just doing what is best. I saw this tactic used in a large chain of California retail stores in the mid-1980s. I read they were closing over a hundred stores. So I approached the firm's executives to ask if I could study their implementation practices. My dissertation research was on organizational death processes in a small sample; I wanted to do a larger study of the differences between how good and bad closings were managed, and this sample seemed perfect. The first meeting with the corporate team that oversaw the closings lasted over an hour, and they were excited to get the project rolling. The retail action team, or, as they jokingly called themselves, "the RAT Patrol," picked four closings they considered to be good and another four they considered bad (largely in terms of the business retained by the company).

I spent several days interviewing the manager and an employee or two at each store. There was a clear pattern: The manager who oversaw each successful closing largely ignored the procedures developed by the retail action team—describing them as cumbersome, ineffective, emotionally insensitive, and out of touch with reality. They developed their own practices instead. One manager held up the thick manual of procedures and policies assembled by the corporate team and bragged that the secret to his success was ignoring the entire thing! He also complained that the RAT Patrol had discouraged him from allowing his people to hold a "wake" for the store, so people could say good-bye to each other. He ignored that advice, too. The executives suggested that the party would stir up anger and resentment. The defiant manager reported that, on the contrary, it was a sweet party that helped people deal with the loss and enabled them to work together better during the final weeks the store remained open.

In contrast, managers in the four bad closings each tried to follow the official procedures closely. All complained that doing so made it difficult to convince customers to transfer their business to other stores and demoralized employees. *Frustration* was the word they used again and again. Customers were frustrated because the procedures were so hard to follow, employees were frustrated because it was so hard to help customers transfer their business, and managers were frustrated and beleaguered because they were being blamed by everyone—including the RAT Patrol—for their store's lousy performance.

When I met with the RAT Patrol after doing these interviews, I began by summarizing the findings, intending to dig into the nuances during the scheduled hour-long meeting. The team leader stood up about three minutes into my talk and announced that something urgent had come up and the meeting couldn't continue. I was quickly marched to the door, and they didn't return my follow-up calls. I guess they didn't want to hear the bad news about their lame practices and procedures and believed it was better to shoot the messenger than to learn about—and fix—the problems.

In contrast to such constructive defiance, I know bosses who employ the opposite strategy to undermine and drive out incompetent superiors. One called it "malicious compliance," following idiotic orders from on high exactly to the letter, thereby assuring the work would suck. This is a risky strategy, of course, but I once had a detailed conversation with a manager at an electronics firm whose team built an ugly and cumbersome product prototype. After it was savaged by the CEO, the manager carefully explained (and documented) that his team had done exactly as the VP of engineering ordered, and although he voiced early and adamant objections to the VP, he gave up because "it was like talking to a brick wall."

So this manager and his team decided: "Let's give him exactly what he wants, so we just said 'Yes sir' and followed his lousy orders precisely." The VP of engineering lost his job as a result. Again, this is a dangerous and destructive strategy, and I would advise any boss to use it only as a last resort.

The Art of Creative Incompetence

Your parents probably taught you that "anything worth doing is worth doing well." Mine sure did. Alas, with all due respect, there are times when smart bosses do a lousy or half-assed job on purpose. They also sometimes encourage their people to join them in doing a crummy job. And such intentional ineptitude is sometimes the best option for enhancing performance and collective humanity. Creative incompetence was popularized by *The Peter Principle* in the 1960s, the wise parody I mentioned earlier. Dr. Peter argued that creative incompetence was the best way to avoid being promoted to one's level of incompetence. He proposed that by choosing to appear incompetent at things that are irrelevant to doing your current job well, your superiors will leap to the false conclusion that *"you have already reached your level of incompetence."* Dr. Peter suggested acts of creative incompetence such as losing irrelevant paperwork now and then, "accidently" parking in the company president's parking space on occasion, dressing slightly shabbily; for women, he advised, "Overly strong perfume or overly brilliant jewelry work well in some cases."

Creative incompetence can be dangerous, as it can be a form of sabotage and can harm people when used in the wrong ways. None of us wants our surgeon or airplane pilot to screw up on purpose when our lives are in their hands. And creative incompetence is unethical when used to lie, steal, or cheat, as was done by the accountants who worked for convicted Ponzi schemer Bernie Madoff. The *New York Times* reported that in pleading guilty, accountant David Friehling essentially "admitted that he had never adequately audited the Madoff operation and, as an

investor in the scheme, had never been a truly independent auditor. Nevertheless, he produced the supposedly
professional and independent audits that sustained the
Madoff fraud year in and year out."

Although it is destructive in the wrong hands, creative
incompetence can be effective and ethical when used in
small doses and with proper precautions. Most bosses are
expected to do so many things that it is often impossible
to perform each chore perfectly—or even very well.
Good bosses focus their attention, and their people's efforts, on the small number of things that matter most.
The best bosses learn when they can and should ignore
the least important demands from others. But some demands can't be avoided even though they have little, if
any, impact on people or performance. In such cases, it
might be wise to do a quick and crummy job so you can
"check the box" and quickly move on to more crucial
chores.

I learned this lesson while Jeff Pfeffer and I were doing
research for *The Knowing-Doing Gap*, when we traveled to
New York to talk with Citibank (now Citigroup) managers
and executives. We had a memorable interview with a fellow whom executives had selected as one of the top performing branch managers in New York City. He told us
that a key to his success was ignoring as many of the unnecessary demands that senior executives imposed on his
branch as possible. He also reported that some demands
could not be ignored, such as completing balanced scorecards for his direct reports. There was no avoiding this

task because these scorecards were among the CEO's pet projects—so compliance was closely monitored. He believed, consistent with the Otis Redding Problem discussed in chapter 5, that it wasn't useful to judge each person on all twenty-five or so dimensions on the scorecard. So he completed the reviews in fast and half-assed ways—then focused his energy on boosting a narrower (and especially crucial) set of performance metrics and on other more vital chores.

Again, creative incompetence must be used with great care, but it is something that every good boss keeps in his or her tool kit. If you are a boss, ask yourself: Are there required (but irrelevant) procedures your people ought to perform in less time-consuming and more half-assed ways? Are there boring or demeaning chores that keep them from doing exciting and more important things? Also consider if your willingness to do low-priority and downright trivial tasks enables other bosses and teams to devote their full attention to more intriguing and crucial challenges. Are there things you are known for doing willingly and well that sap time from work that is more important to your people, your organization, and your own career? For example, do you seem to lead every time-sucking but insignificant task force and organize every holiday party (because no one else will or they always screw it up)? Are you entertaining a constant parade of visitors whom other bosses don't believe are worth wasting time with? If you can't wiggle out of such chores, perhaps it is time for a bit of creative incompetence.

Slay—Or at Least Slow—Their Enemies

Every group I've ever been part of, or known well, believes there is some person or group who is out to get them or make their lives miserable. Sociologists will tell you that feeling besieged by an enemy has an upside, as it brings people together to fight the common threat. Ann Rhoades, former head of the People Department at Southwest Airlines, described to me how a fellow executive earned the loyalty of Southwest gate agents by interrupting a nasty and abusive passenger, telling the jerk that he couldn't allow his people to be treated that way, and then marching him to an American Airlines gate to buy him a ticket to send him on his way. This not only brought Southwest people together because they felt protected, it brought them together because American was seen as an evil competitor that deserved that asshole passenger.

Good bosses don't just protect their people from destructive and despised outsiders. They protect their people from enemies up the chain, especially bosses who undermine their charges' ability to get work done and make them miserable. Consider a police sergeant in Texas who showed extraordinary courage in bringing his abusive boss down a notch. As reported on my blog, it started when his boss gave him a copy of *The No Asshole Rule*:

> I was given your book by my supervisor to read so
> we could "discuss" leadership ideas. I thought this was

a little odd as I could best describe the leadership style of my boss as leadership by oppression. I began to read the book, reluctantly I might add as I believed he was giving me a not so subtle hint, and realized that he had made a colossal mistake. The mistake being that not only could the examples of "assholeness" in the book fit my boss, but it armed me in dealing with him. To be sure, I did learn ways to keep myself in check with the inner asshole that sometimes comes out in my line of work. The result of reading this book actually had me telling him, in front of eight of my subordinates that I supervise, that his behavior of verbally berating officers was not acceptable on my shift. I actually said to him, "It's your fault! You gave me *The No Asshole Rule* book!" Boy it felt good.

My advice, by the way, is that if you are going to do something this public and risky, you better have a lot of job security, a lot of powerful friends, or another job offer. Embarrassing your crummy boss is a good way to get yourself fired in many places.

Battle for Resources

To succeed at their jobs, your people need the right materials and tools, and enough money. I love reading about Robert Townsend's overbearing efforts to get his people resources. We already saw how he fought for higher pay for his people at American Express. Townsend also carried a letter of resignation around with him, which he shoved in many bureaucrats' faces (and asked them to cosign) when they wouldn't cough up the equipment or other resources his people needed. His antics were entertaining, but taking such extreme steps can get you fired in some places and, in others, earn you the reputation as an asshole who doesn't deserve to be rewarded for such theatrics. In most places, it is wiser to be more subtle and civilized, but to fight for your people just as hard.

To illustrate: Corey Billington, who we met in chapter 1, was constantly battling to get his people what they needed to succeed. He gently, but persistently, battled away to get his people more competitive salaries, a larger budget to hire more professionals and supply-chain experts, and get more space. Corey also knew that little things can mean a lot, and as a boss, you can earn credibility with your people by demonstrating that you will go to war for them every now and then—even over fairly trivial things.

The donuts at SPaM are a great example. A few years after Corey became boss, HP instituted a host of cost-cutting moves, and one of the changes was that although employees got free donuts every morning for decades, they were being eliminated to save money. Corey's people were remarkably pissed off that corporate was taking away their donuts! They were all working very long hours and had hard evidence they were saving the company a lot of money, and they felt they ought to be rewarded rather than punished for their success. So Corey struck a deal with corporate that he would use SPaM's own budget to pay for the donuts. I was frankly dumbfounded by how happy everyone was about the donut victory. I remember sitting in the break room right after it happened. One employee after another came in and bragged about the donuts, that "we earned the right to keep them." They saw Corey's victory as a blow against corporate in defense of their pride and dignity—and as recognition of their performance. We human beings are quirky creatures, something that no boss should ever forget.

Take the Heat for Their Mistakes

One executive I work with—who leads an organization composed mostly of men—described how one of her employees made a big mistake that cost the company a lot of money. She didn't blame him when the board of directors started going after her for the costly error. Instead, she accepted responsibility and endured some pretty nasty criticism. As she put it, "I let him hide behind my skirt because when you are the boss, part of your job is to protect your people when they screw up."

This means of shielding people is painful but often effective. Bosses who take the heat for their people build loyalty—when you take the heat for someone's errors, they definitely owe you. If they don't realize it, make sure that they get the message somehow. Also, as we saw, people need to feel safe to learn new things, take risks, and act without undue fear. Taking the heat makes clear that you aren't just spewing out hollow rhetoric about making it safe for people. Finally, you might as well step up and take the blame when something goes wrong. As research on the romance of leadership shows, since you are the boss you are going to get it anyway. But don't just apologize for the mistake and silently endure the slings and arrows. Figure out what you learned so you can avoid making the mistake again, announce and implement the resulting lessons, and in doing so reinforce beliefs that you control the fate of your team or organization.

The Better Your Boss and Your Organization, the Less You Need to Shield People

These tactics for shielding your followers from destructive people and practices are necessary evils in most organizations. But the better your boss is, the less you need to shield your people from external idiocy interference and inefficiency. One of my favorite bosses ever is Annette Kyle, who managed sixty or so employees at a loading terminal for the Celanese Corporation in Bayport, Texas. Annette led what she called a "revolution" that entailed massive changes in the operation. These included bringing in different equipment, changing people's titles and responsibilities, revamping the measurement system so the location of ships, railcars, and trucks headed for the terminal were transparent to everyone, repairing the emotional tone (Annette sewed No Whining patches on their uniforms), and revamping her own job, too (she auctioned off her desk to the workers because "I shouldn't be sitting behind a desk; I should be out helping you"). The results included a drop in demurrage fees (charges paid when a ship arrived and they weren't ready to load it) from 2.5 million dollars the year before the revolution to less than ten thousand dollars the year after. Before the change, it took workers an average of over three hours to load a truck once it arrived. After the revolution, over 90 percent of trucks were loaded within one hour. Surveys and interviews showed that employees were more satisfied with their jobs after the change and were proud of what they had accomplished together, and only one employee quit during the first year of the change.

When I asked Annette how she got away with making such radical changes in her little corner of the giant corporation, she answered that her boss protected her almost completely from the senior management—he dug up resources and brought in experts to help her, but never discussed the revolution at Bayport with top executives until it was a rousing success. Annette's boss made it possible for her and her people to implement sweeping changes with little interference from on high.

Similarly, the better managed your organization is, the less you will need to use this stuff. Skilled bosses don't have to shield their people as much at well-run places as they do at badly run places. At Amazon.com, for example, bosses take little heat when their people try things that fail or when their people act without first asking for permission. Amazon's most prestigious employee award is called the "Just Do It." Employees win it from CEO Jeff Bezos for taking actions to help the company and doing so without getting their boss's permission first. Employees don't need much protection from above under these conditions. As a rule, the less idiocy that rains down from above, the less shielding a good boss needs to do.

CHAPTER 7

Don't Shirk the Dirty Work

Every boss must do things that upset and hurt people. If you are the boss, it is your job to issue reprimands, fire people, deny budget requests, transfer employees to jobs they don't want, and implement mergers, layoffs, and shutdowns. If you can't or won't perform such unpleasant chores, perhaps you shouldn't be the boss. Or, if you still want the job, you better recruit someone else to do your dirty work.

The best bosses don't delay or duck difficult deeds. Consider a study by Charles O'Reilly and Barton Weitz on how supervisors handled problematic sales employees— those with poor productivity, lack of punctuality, bad attitudes, and other misdeeds. Bosses of the most productive work groups confronted problems directly and quickly, issued more warnings and formal punishments, and promptly fired employees when warnings failed. These no-nonsense bosses inspired team performance because their words and actions made crystal clear that they would not tolerate crummy work.

Lousy bosses live in a fantasyland of denial and delusion. They are remarkably adept at inventing excuses for putting off gut-wrenching work. They may talk tough but lack the courage to confront employees with negative feedback, punishments, or other bad news. One company had a trio of executives who persistently pounded the table and insisted on firing mediocre performers—often over objections by fellow executives that these employees' problems were temporary or reversible. The tough talkers sometimes got their way by volunteering to do the firings themselves. Then, weeks slipped by as the macho table pounders delayed these difficult conversations. Meanwhile, rumors raged that the targeted employees had been canned and they wondered and worried why bosses were avoiding them. On several occasions, the same executives who opposed the firings felt compelled to end the uncertainty, so they stepped up and did the deed for their bellicose but spineless colleagues.

Bosses sometimes initiate dirty work because they believe it is the right thing to do. When Ann Rhoades was head of the People Department at Southwest Airlines, she helped make the decision to fire fellow executive David Neeleman, who had joined Southwest as part of a merger with Morris Air. Neeleman's quarreling and complaining about Southwest were undermining the dynamics of the senior team, along with their famously warm and cooperative culture. Ann agreed that Neeleman had to go and helped break the bad news to him.

Other times, bosses are asked to implement decisions they disagree with and may have openly opposed. But they don't keep battling the decision or quit. They realize there are times when it is wisest to do a *good job of implementing a bad decision*. I was working with PeopleSoft when they faced a hostile takeover bid from software giant Oracle, which eventually bought and absorbed the company. One PeopleSoft manager (I'll call her "Cindy") vehemently opposed the takeover. Yet, after it was inevitable, Cindy worked to protect and respect her team of twenty or so employees. She made a time line of upcoming events for them and acknowledged facts she didn't know (or couldn't talk about). Cindy kept her team's spirits up until they were disbanded by doing little things like celebrating birthdays, listening to people cry and vent (but asking them not to slip into cynicism), and joking about why Larry Ellison (Oracle's controversial CEO) really wasn't such a bad guy after all.

The upshot is there are times when every boss must do things that hurt others. *But there is a big difference between what you do and how you do it.* Ann Rhoades's history with David Neeleman illustrates the point: He wasn't happy about getting fired, but Neeleman was sufficiently impressed with how Ann handled this and other chores at Southwest that he hired her as head of human resources several years later when he founded JetBlue Airways.

Research by behavioral scientists shows that dirty work

does less harm when bosses add four antidotes into the mix: Prediction, Understanding, Control, and Compassion. I identified the first three with Robert Kahn, my mentor at the University of Michigan. There was a recession in Michigan in the early 1980s, and we were struck by how differently the best versus the worst managers dealt with layoffs, pay cuts and other painful changes. The best found ways to help people predict what would happen, understand why, and control how events unfolded. Jeff Pfeffer and I later added compassion, following evidence that good bosses express empathy and warmth when delivering bad news and implementing change.

Predictability

The worst bosses condemn their people to live in constant fear as they wait for the next wave of bad news, which always seems to hit without warning and at random intervals. The best bosses do everything possible to communicate when and how distressing events will unfold. When the timing of a stressful event can be predicted, so can its absence: Psychologist Martin Seligman called this the safety signal hypothesis. Predictability helps people know when to relax versus when dread and vigilance are warranted—which protects them from the emotional and physical exhaustion that results when people never feel safe from harm for even a moment. Seligman illustrated his hypothesis with air-raid sirens used during the German bombing of London during

World War II. The sirens were so reliable that people went about their lives most of the time without fear; they didn't need to worry about dashing to the shelters unless the sirens sounded.

The safety signal hypothesis also applies to less catastrophic threats like pay cuts, layoffs, mergers, and closings. The CEO of a troubled nonprofit organization used it in a heads-up memo to his staff: He explained that pay cuts and layoffs might be necessary if the stock market and donations failed to rebound. The CEO also made a commitment: No pay cuts or layoffs would happen for at least three months. So people knew they were safe at least until then. At another company, managers did deeper job cuts than were immediately necessary because they wanted to avoid inflicting another round of layoffs on their distraught and distracted people for as long as possible. After the cuts, they announced that no more would occur for at least six months. This strategy is bolstered by research showing that surviving multiple rounds of layoffs wears down people's psychological defenses, provoking depression, health problems, and thoughts of quitting. More broadly, bosses who expose people to shorter, fewer, and more predictable rounds of distress promote both performance and humanity.

Predictability is all about creating realistic expectations. But how people react to bad news isn't just shaped by expectations the boss sets for the future. Your personal history as a boss and your organization's history shape expectations about whether dirty work will be construed as reasonable or not—regardless of what you say right now. Unfortunately, the *better* you and your organization have treated people in the past, the *worse* they will react to the same bad news. Christopher Zatzick and Roderick Iverson's study of three thousand Canadian workplaces found that layoffs had the worst effects on productivity in "high involvement" organizations—which emphasized treating people humanely and employee participation more than traditional workplaces did. A key lesson is that when bosses take harsher actions than in the past, they need damn good answers to the question: "Why are you doing this to us now?"

Understanding

We human beings can't help wondering why things happen, even when all that cogitating doesn't change our fates. We are obsessed with and comforted by explanations— especially for distressing and destructive events. When people have no information, they fill the vacuum by inventing and spreading false and often frightening explanations. This penchant for wondering why (and assuming the worst) means the explanations imagined by uninformed employees are typically more dire and less flattering to bosses than the unvarnished truth. The best bosses know it is better to give people explanations they dislike than no explanation at all. More than fifty studies show that when employees are given sound and believable explanations for unsettling changes like pay cuts, layoffs, and mergers, they are less prone to become angry and anxious, retaliate, quit, steal, or become less productive.

The virtues of careful explanations are seen in research on how employees in two (nearly identical) manufacturing plants responded to unwelcome and unexpected news: Their parent corporation was merging with another big company. David Schweiger and Angelo Denisi surveyed employees right after the announcement and found that it provoked widespread dissatisfaction, stress, and distrust in both plants. Employees were especially freaked out when executives informed them "redundant facilities and jobs would have to be eliminated" to achieve "economies of scale." The two plants produced identical products, were roughly the same size, and had similar workforces. But there were big differences in how the corporate leaders communicated after the scary announcement. In one plant, employees received only vague communications during the subsequent three months. In the second, an extensive communication program was implemented. The plant manager met every week with supervisors and employees in each department to make announcements and answer questions. The plant published a weekly newsletter with updates about the merger and had a hotline to answer employees' questions. The plant manager also met privately with employees to inform them when decisions (such as transfers or layoffs) were made about their fate.

As the program kicked in, employees in the "high communication" plant felt more secure about their jobs, less stressed, more committed, and reported superior job performance—while no such improvements occurred at the other plant. The lesson is that even when bosses can't stop bad things from happening to people, less damage results when they carefully explain what will happen and why. This study also shows that bolstering understanding can unleash the other three antidotes. Management's quick and detailed responses to employees' questions helped them predict what was ahead. These answers also often contained information about how employees could help themselves, enabling them to take some control over their lives. And the private meetings executives had with employees about their fates conveyed compassion, concern, and respect.

Another lesson echoes the discussion of "*Sesame Street* Simple" in chapter 5: When people are freaked out, skilled bosses make their explanations as simple as possible and repeat them over and over—and do so through multiple communication channels. When fear is in the air, your mantra should be: Simple, Concrete, Credible, and Repetitive. This mantra is even necessary when delivering good news to people braced for bad news. The CEO of one software company told me that he sent an e-mail to all his employees emphasizing that—unlike many companies in Silicon Valley at the time—they weren't doing any layoffs. In fact, he told them, the company would be growing the workforce by about 20 percent in the coming year. Yet, because so many employees had friends who recently had lost jobs at places like Google and Yahoo!, they had trouble hearing or believing the good news. People asked again and again,

"When are the layoffs coming?" The CEO then went on a campaign to repeat the news there would be no layoffs, the company was doing great, and would be hiring—in one-on-ones, group meetings, and e-mails. He even shared the company's bank statements in a second e-mail to every employee, as he explained, "so they can understand where our assets are and how safe they are." Eventually, the message got through. This story demonstrates how when fear is in the air, people have trouble hearing the facts and are prone to assuming the worst, even when things are going well.

Control

As we've seen, great bosses help followers feel powerful rather than powerless—especially during rough times. Chapter 1 emphasized that the best bosses work with their charges to spot and implement small wins. Recall the CEO who used this strategy when his people started freaking out about a sales campaign that was crucial to the company's survival. He calmed and focused his team by having them break down the campaign into specific tasks, divide the list into easy and hard tasks, and then make quick progress on the easy ones. This strategy transformed a situation where people felt overwhelmed and helpless into one where, after accomplishing a string of small wins, *they felt a strong link between their actions and meaningful changes around them*—which is how behavioral scientists define the perception of control.

Research on control has been conducted under many different banners—self-efficacy, autonomy, helplessness, empowerment, and, of course, small wins. The jargon varies, but study after study shows that when people experience some control over their lives, they enjoy better physical and mental health. Even when people can't control their ultimate fates, their well-being improves when they can influence some aspects of their lives. For bosses, this means your dirty work will do less harm if you can give people some control over *when* and *how* bad things happen to them. I once worked with a firm that enforced infamously tough performance standards, routinely forcing out 10 to 20 percent of its people per year. Yet nearly every former employee I met admired the firm, remembered their time there fondly, and harbored little if any hostility toward their ex-bosses. I also never met a current employee who worried constantly about the high probability of getting sacked in a few years—or sooner. One reason people didn't go nuts was that after bosses gave employees gentle but clear signals that their days were numbered, they devoted a great deal of effort to talking with employees about what they wanted to do next and how the firm could help make it happen. Although people had no choice about leaving the firm, they suffered far less than fired employees elsewhere because they had considerable control over where they went next, how they left, and (within reason) when they would leave.

Compassion

The worst bosses not only make followers feel vulnerable and weak during hard times, they also demean, humiliate, and piss them off. Customer support specialist Mark Eckley was stunned when his bosses informed one hundred of his coworkers they were being sacked immediately, then had security guards march them out the door. He reported, "It was pretty sickening to watch." Worse yet, his bosses immediately started bad-mouthing fired employees. Even though Mark wasn't fired, he was angry and scared, and he left for another job a few months later.

In England, Katy Tanner was hurt and outraged by a text message from her boss at the Blue Banana, a body-piercing studio: "We've reviewed your sales figures and they're not really up to the level we need." He added, "As a result, we will not require your services any more. Thank you for your time with us." A company spokesperson defended this means of firing Ms. Tanner. He explained that using text messages was part of Blue Banana's "youth culture," so when they found she wasn't answering her phone, "we wished to spare Miss Tanner the embarrassment and expense of coming into the store only to be sent straight home again, it was decided this was the best course of action to take." A colder approach was used to sack four hundred RadioShack employees at the company's Fort Worth headquarters. They were notified via an impersonal e-mail: "The work force reduction notification is currently in progress" and "Unfortunately your position is one that has been eliminated." The company had held meetings in which management warned people that layoffs were coming and those who lost jobs would be notified via e-mail rather than face-to-face. Yet as Professor Derrick D'Souza, of the University of North Texas, wondered, "If I put myself in their shoes, I'd say, 'Didn't they have a few minutes to tell me?'"

The damage that clueless and coldhearted bosses can do was captured in a reader's report on my blog about an HR executive who bungled "the inevitable layoffs" after a merger: "He did them in a glass-walled conference room in the middle of the office, so that for hours every time someone went to the bathroom or got a cup of coffee, they walked by a big glass box containing someone getting canned, often crying, etc." Perhaps the winner of this race to the bottom was a manager at the Dean Health System in Wisconsin, who removed a nurse from the operating room in the middle of a procedure to tell her that she was fired. Dean's head of communication later confessed this method reflected "an error in judgment" and a violation of medical protocol—and emphasized that the offending manager was "extremely remorseful." I hope so, but I wonder what compelled the manager to do something so clueless and cruel in the first place.

In contrast, the best bosses convey empathy as they make and implement tough decisions—which bolsters performance and humanity. Consider how executives at Martha Stewart Living Omnimedia dismissed employees when closing their catalog business. Vice President Ron Thomas warned managers that "they weren't going to sleep the night before" the layoffs. He urged them, "Try to envision that one day you may be on the other side of the table—so you should treat people the way you'd like to be treated in this situation." Thomas told the *Wall Street Journal*, "We make sure people who are losing a job know someone will call them to start helping them within a day." Thomas called everyone he knew at other catalog businesses to see if they had openings. This compassion helped both those who lost jobs and those who remained to get through the rough patch, and helped Martha Stewart recruit better talent down the road. As Thomas put it, "If you handle a restructuring well, the word gets out that you're a good place to work. If we post a job opening today, we'll get 1,500 resumes tomorrow."

The power of compassion is seen in Jerald Greenberg's research on insomnia among nurses. Insomnia has been linked to numerous health problems including heart disease, memory loss, and depression. The errors, accidents, and lost productivity linked to insomnia among U.S. workers costs over 100 billion dollars a year. Greenberg followed 322 nurses who got pay cuts (averaging about 10 percent) for forty weeks. During the first weeks after the cut, nurses reported big spikes in sleep problems—trouble falling and staying asleep and waking up feeling worn out. Then nineteen supervisors who oversaw about half (158) of these nurses were trained to give better interpersonal and informational support—while supervisors of the other 164 nurses received no training. The training included cases, discussions, and role-playing to teach supervisors how to treat followers with respect, be accessible, listen to concerns, and "communicate details in a timely manner and tailor them to individuals." In other words, supervisors were taught the art of compassion (and to provide prediction and understanding, too). The nurses with trained supervisors reported a pronounced drop in sleep problems within a month—while sleep problems continued among nurses with untrained supervisors. A six-month follow-up revealed that these differences persisted. There was little improvement in the sleep problems suffered by nurses with untrained supervisors. But nurses with trained supervisors continued to improve and slept nearly as well as before the cuts. And more than twice as many nurses (44 vs. 20) with untrained rather than trained supervisors had resigned.

Greenberg also shows that when bosses lack compassion, employees even the score. He studied pay cuts in two manufacturing plants. In the plant where executives announced the cuts in a cold and curt way (and gave incomplete explanations), the subsequent theft rate was nearly twice as high compared to the plant where executives gave complete and compassionate explanations for the cuts. Greenberg also studied a retail store that taught supervisors to be fair and compassionate. Before the intervention, employees saw bosses as "disrespectful, uncaring, and insensitive." Afterwards, employee attitudes improved markedly and thefts dropped by about 50 percent. One salesperson reported, "[My supervisor] used to be a real SOB, and I hated working for him, and I stole every chance I got. Now, he is so kind to me, I'd feel bad about taking anything."

Diagnostic Questions for Dirty Work

1. Is It Necessary?

There are certainly times when punishment, demotions, layoffs, and other tough moves are most effective. Yet, before assuming they are necessary, creative bosses consider if a different path is better. In March 2009, CEO Paul Levy of the Beth Israel Deaconess Medical Center in Boston was concerned that layoffs would be required among his eight thousand employees because of the financial downturn. He gathered hundreds of employees and said: "I want to run an idea by you.... I'd like to do what we can to protect the lower-wage earners—the transporters, the housekeepers, the food service people. A lot of these people work really hard, and I don't want to put an additional burden on them. Now, if we protect these workers, it means the rest of us will have to make a bigger sacrifice." He continued, "It means that others will have to give up more of their salary or benefits."

The *Boston Globe* reported, "He had barely gotten the words out of his mouth when Sherman Auditorium erupted in applause. Thunderous, heartfelt, sustained applause."

Hundreds of suggestions poured in from employees via e-mail: "A nurse said her floor voted unanimously to forgo a 3 percent raise. A guy in finance who got laid off from his last job at a hospital in Rhode Island suggested working one less day a week. Another nurse said she was willing to give up some vacation and sick time. A respiratory therapist suggested eliminating bonuses." Dozens of these suggestions were implemented, and the round of layoffs was averted.

The discomfort with layoffs at Beth Israel Deaconess stemmed from the compassion that Paul Levy and his colleagues had for coworkers at the bottom of the hospital's hierarchy. Yet there is also a strong business case against using layoffs as a knee-jerk response in even the most profit-hungry places. Research by the management consulting firm Bain suggests that when a downturn hits, companies that use layoffs last and least recover more quickly and hold a competitive advantage when good times return. Bain's study of S&P 500 firms found that it takes twelve to eighteen months before companies begin to reap the financial benefits from layoffs because of severance costs and negative effects on surviving workers. Often, before the savings kick in, the economy starts to rebound and the company is forced to hire people much like those fired. The Bain researchers concluded that although widely used, this "binge and purge" approach is a bad way to control labor costs.

The lesson is: before taking a tough action, ask yourself, "Am I doing this because it is the right thing, or because it is what we've always done here or what everyone else does in other organizations?"

2. Do You Have the Power to Do It Right?

Unfortunately, sometimes bosses who have every justification to use tough tactics realize they simply lack the power to do it right—that doing the dirty work is impossible, will have no effect, or will backfire and kill productivity and cooperation. This predicament is sometimes faced by bosses who lead employees with massive job security (e.g., those protected by labor unions or government regulations). It also happens to administrators who are cat herders rather than authority figures in places like universities, hospitals, and law firms, who often have weak influence over professionals like professors, physicians, and partners. When, for practical reasons, it is difficult or impossible to punish employee misdeeds or remove poor performers, imaginative bosses sometimes still find ways to persuade people to change their destructive ways.

Consider a strange program that eliminated theft at a sawmill employing about 1,200 workers—most protected by a powerful union. Employee theft was costing the mill about a million dollars a year. Yet management felt powerless to stop it. When one supervisor tried to stop employees from leaving with "what appeared to be very heavy lunch boxes" it unleashed such a deluge of grievances that the plant's HR manager pleaded with him to drop the matter. Supervisors soon adopted the slogan "Hear no evil, see no evil."

This pathetic powerlessness persisted until Professor Gary Latham was brought in to interview employees. The workers revealed they were ripping off the company simply because it was fun and challenging—they didn't actually need most of the stuff. One worker described the thrill of stealing something called a head rig (it weighed over a ton) and bragging about it to his buddies. Management threatened to install a video surveillance system to catch thieves, but rather than getting angry, workers got even more excited because stealing the video equipment would be such fun. Even though monitoring, punishment, and firings were certainly justified, the mill's management lacked the power to do such dirty work.

Latham and the plant managers decided a more promising solution was to *kill the thrill*. Management introduced a library system where employees could borrow the same equipment they had been stealing. Theft dropped to virtually zero immediately and remained there as Latham followed the plant for the next three years. The thrill was gone; stealing something you could get for free wasn't anything to brag about. Management also introduced an amnesty program, where employees could return equipment without punishment. Employees were told that when they returned it, management would assume they were doing a favor for an anonymous friend. Employees started returning equipment by the truckload, in part because their wives were irritated by how much space it took up in garages, sheds, and backyards. So they pressed their husbands to return the stuff.

This intervention is intriguing because, rather than fighting a losing battle against the peer culture, plant management neutered the root cause. They killed the thrill with generosity and forgiveness. The lesson is that when bosses don't have the power to do dirty work right, figuring out the cause of bad behavior and trying something creative rather than punitive may be the most promising path—no matter how much the perpetrators may deserve to be punished and sent packing.

3. Is the Peer Culture on Your Side?

All bosses can be more effective when they work with, rather than against, the peer culture. Bosses who are known as fair and consistent will get more support from the peer culture when they do their dirty work. Research on punishment shows that coworkers often believe that offenders are let off too easily by bosses—especially when they have violated the rules consistently, shown little remorse, and a fair process was used to convict and punish the wrongdoer. In the best workplaces, bosses and their charges agree on what is right and wrong, and peers—not the boss—dish out punishment. Research on employee theft shows that ridicule, ostracism, and nasty gossip by peers is 250 percent more effective for deterring stealing than formal punishment by supervisors.

Peer power can backfire, however, when bosses define

correct behavior differently from their followers. The key to breaking through, as the sawmill story shows, is to identify why peers are condoning bad behavior and to remove the cause. Sometimes, problems can be traced to ringleaders. Other times, problems are so ingrained that it is best to disband the group or organization and start over. But before taking extreme action, remember that simple steps can be remarkably effective. In a Swedish grocery store, management simply started posting lists in the employee's break room of items stolen by employees. They reminded employees that the costs were passed on to customers, and the lost income made it difficult to raise their pay. Theft dropped dramatically, apparently because employees started policing each other more.

There are also times when a peer culture is broken because the boss hasn't set the right expectations with influential members. University of Michigan football coach Bo Schembechler admitted that such a failure cost his team a national championship one year. Bo believed his 1980 team was the most talented he coached during his twenty years at Michigan, but their chances to win the title evaporated after losing a supposedly easy game to South Carolina. Bo then learned there was dissension among his players, and many were complaining about working too hard. As former Ford CEO Donald Petersen tells it, when Bo talked to the team captain, "the kid admitted that he was one of those complaining and said he thought a number of things were being handled the wrong way." Bo didn't get mad: "He realized that he'd never once called the captain aside and explained why the hard work was necessary and how important his role was—that the whole team would take their lead from his view of the coaching staff, the importance of discipline, and so on." After Bo started having these conversations with the captain, the player became a positive force, the grumbling stopped, and Michigan went undefeated the rest of the year.

4. Are You Living in a Fool's Paradise?

If you, as the boss, believe that you are doing splendid dirty work, stop patting yourself on the back and figure out if you are deluding yourself. Just because you fancy yourself as fair and humane does not mean your people see it that way. As we saw with research on the toxic tandem, bosses often have an overly positive and incomplete picture of how followers respond to their moves. Research on workplace discipline is instructive here: Managers who dish out punishment usually believe their reprimands or suspensions improve bad employee behavior and create few, if any, adverse effects. But punished employees often vehemently disagree with their bosses' rosy reports and turn into alienated and angry backstabbers.

Leanne Atwater and her colleagues interviewed a call center employee who was given a strong reprimand from his boss for slacking off. The employee admitted: "The discipline scared a lot of us into not doing it anymore." This boss had good reason to believe the punishment was effective, but she did not realize that it had also unleashed simmering rage. The employee seethed and threatened, "Someday down the road I just want to get her back and make her pay for it."

As a boss, you can't always know (let alone control) how people react to you. Yet because people often fear and sometimes respect authority figures, the safest assumptions are that your judgments are flawed and excessively optimistic, and that people (worried you will shoot the messenger) won't deliver bad news to you. I learned this lesson early in my career at Stanford, when I was assigned to teach an 8:00 AM class. Most college students stay up late, so they despise early classes and arrive late. I devised a little system to motivate students to arrive on time: If they missed the starting time, I made them wait in the hall with fellow latecomers. When I came to a reasonable break point, usually about ten minutes into class, I allowed the (typically six or seven) stragglers to take their seats.

I thought the system was working great. Just to make sure, after three weeks or so, I engaged the class in a discussion of my tardiness control system. Of the seventy-five or so students in my class, only two or three spoke up. Each offered tepid praise. After class, my course assistant, Dave Jalajas, said to me something like "Bob, I hate to tell you this, but they are afraid to tell you the truth...they hate it." In the next class, I passed out an anonymous survey about the system. I was shocked to find that *every single student reported hating the system and wanted it abandoned immediately.* I got rid of the despised system and went to a more subtle approach where Dave wrote down names of latecomers. I also learned a lesson about how

differently things looked just because I had a little power—
and how my charges were afraid to look me in the eye and
tell me how they really felt.

5. Is That Lie Worth Telling?

Research on everything from negotiation, to revenge, to
company integrity reveals that when people believe they
are dealing with a liar (or a pack of them), they get angry,
retaliate by bad-mouthing them and withholding effort, and
lose faith in otherwise competent bosses and colleagues.
One executive I worked with described how her company's
executive team went through weeks of turmoil while their
CEO was rumored to be in the running for the top job
at a larger company. During executive team meetings, the
CEO repeatedly went out of his way to deny interest in the
other job—although, in fact, he had been a candidate
the entire time. When the CEO didn't get the job, he went to
the press (before talking to anyone on his team) to say that
lest anyone think he hadn't been offered the job, he had
actually withdrawn from the process.

While this move protected his public brand, it angered
and confused his team, as they had believed his prior deni-
als. Matters got worse when the CEO stood up at an all-
hands meeting and told hundreds of employees that he had
considered accepting the job (which wasn't offered) but de-
clined it because he loved them so much and didn't want to
be anywhere else. Whatever the motivation for these lies, the
CEO's actions eroded trust and led many on his executive

team to think about finding newer, bigger roles, too. Within eighteen months, the entire team had left the company.

As we've seen, what you as a boss have done in the past colors how people respond to the moves you make. Once people believe you are a liar, all the authentic prediction, understanding, control, and compassion in the world may not be enough to save you—or your organization—from the fury and vengeance provoked by your past sins.

6. Can You Keep Your Big Mouth Shut?

Dirty work requires discretion. When bosses are trying to decide, say, how to deal with poor performers, implement mergers, or schedule layoffs, open and indiscreet discussions can backfire. Initial conversations among decision makers are often best done in small groups by circumspect people. Involving too many stakeholders too early stifles frank discussion and argument. People can be hurt, and laws broken, as secret business strategies or layoff lists leak out to the organization or public. A partner at a large law firm, Pillsbury Winthrop Shaw Pittman, provides a cautionary tale about the damage and embarrassment that can result from such indiscretions. As mentioned in the preface, in February 2009, one of the firm's partners was talking loudly on his cell phone as he rode on a train. A fellow passenger figured out who the partner was and that he was talking about impending layoffs at the firm. That passenger then wrote on a blog:

I, along with all of the other passengers, was sitting quietly when the man directly behind me decided to make a phone call using his Bluetooth. He was talking so loudly that I think most people in the car were able to hear him....His conversation, though he stressed how necessary it was to be kept secret [ah, the irony], detailed the current plans of Pillsbury to lay off somewhere in the range of 15–20 attorneys from four offices by the end of March, including a few senior associates with low billable hours and two or three first-year associates.

To Pillsbury's credit, after this story was picked up by the press, they admitted it: "We apologize for the unfortunate manner in which our deliberations about reductions have become public." They also acknowledged, "We will be implementing reductions." The lesson is that although there is a time for open communication of facts, destructive rumors (and facts) can fly and people can be damaged by bosses who can't keep their big mouths shut.

7. Do You Need a Bad Cop?

I once had a long "therapy session" with a former student who had done such a great job as an engineer that he was promoted to team leader. But he only lasted a few months because, as he said, "My boss kept telling me that my team was screwing around too much, that a good boss kicks butt when necessary. I couldn't do that to my friends, so I asked for a demotion." I admire this engineer because he realized that, as they say in *The Peter Principle*, he had risen to the level of incompetence and asked to be demoted down to his level of competence.

Another way to solve this problem is to treat being the boss as a team effort. If you can't do the dirty work, recruit a bad cop to do it for you. That is apparently how the famous chef Alice Waters gets her dirty work done. Alice runs Chez Panisse, a restaurant in Berkeley, California, where—as founder and executive chef—she helped start a movement in American cooking that emphasizes fresh, local, and organic ingredients. Thomas McNamee's biography shows how, during the nearly forty years that Alice has led Chez Panisse, her love of people and food has infected those around her. Along the way, however, many employees have been fired at Chez Panisse (apparently always with Alice's approval). Business partner Greil Marcus reports such cuts have been made with "utter ruthlessness and boldness." But Alice herself doesn't wield the axe. One of her colleagues usually gently hints to the targeted person that Alice isn't "entirely pleased." If such hints don't drive the person out, one of Alice's colleagues then does the firing. The lesson is that, if you can't bring yourself to do dirty work, work with a bad cop; and if you love being tough (but compassion isn't your thing), team up with a good cop.

Beware: The Revenge Trap

The accompanying "12 Commandments of Bosses' Dirty Work" summarize the central ideas in this chapter. The eleventh commandment stems from an unfortunate side effect of doing dirty work: No matter how necessary it may be, the people your actions hurt sometimes battle back—and may do so in mean-spirited, irrational, and humiliating ways. As a boss, keeping your anger and vindictiveness in check isn't easy in the heat of the moment. But once your main motive for dirty work is to exact revenge, rather than to promote collective performance and humanity, you risk becoming an incompetent asshole. Fighting to defend yourself is necessary and noble, and if you are not overly vindictive and unfair, chances are your bosses, peers, and direct reports will understand—and if you are lucky (or, better yet, have always had *their* backs), they will jump in to defend you. But once you sink to the level of those who attack you (or lower), you risk getting sucked into a vicious circle of revenge. Beware if you are constantly seething with rage, believe that every slight must be avenged, or travel through life doing harm and being harmed—but are never satisfied that the score is settled.

Finally, the best bosses master the fine art of emotional detachment. They learn to forgive people who lash out at them, especially those hurt by their dirty work. And they learn to forgive themselves, too. Forgiveness is not only useful for breaking out of the vicious circle of revenge, but people who let go of their anger also enjoy better mental health, have lower heart rates and blood pressure, and sleep better.

THE 12 COMMANDMENTS OF BOSSES' DIRTY WORK

How to Implement Tough Decisions in Effective and Humane Ways

1. Do not delay painful decisions and actions; hoping the problem will go away or that someone else will do your dirty work rarely is an effective path.
2. Assume that you are clueless, or at least have only a dim understanding, of how people judge you and the dirty work that you do.
3. Implement tough decisions as well as you can—even if they strike you as wrong or misguided. Or get out of the way and let someone else do it.
4. Do everything possible to communicate to all who will be affected how distressing events will unfold, so they can *predict* when bad things will (and will not) happen to them.
5. Explain early and often *why* the dirty work is necessary.
6. Look for ways to give employees influence over *how* painful changes happen to them, even when it is impossible to change *what* will happen to them.
7. Never humiliate, belittle, or bad-mouth people who are the targets of your dirty work.
8. Ask yourself and fellow bosses to seriously consider if the dirty work is really necessary before implementing it. Just because all your competitors do it, or you have always done it in the past, does not mean it is wise right now.
9. Do not bullshit or lie to employees, as doing so can destroy their loyalty and confidence, along with your reputation.

10. Keep your big mouth shut. Divulging sensitive or confidential information can harm employees, your organization, and you, too.
11. Refrain from doing mean-spirited things to exact personal revenge against employees who resist or object to your dirty work.
12. Do not attempt dirty work if you lack the power to do it right, no matter how necessary it may seem.

CHAPTER 8

Squelch Your Inner Bosshole

If a team of world-class behavioral scientists designed a job that was optimized for turning occupants into assholes, the result would be disturbingly similar to many, if not most, bosses' jobs. As we will see, common features of these jobs—power, performance pressure, and exhaustion—provoke bosses to leave followers feeling disrespected, emotionally damaged, and de-energized. These forces help explain why bosses are to blame for the lion's share of workplace bullying and abuse. A 2007 Zogby survey, using a representative U.S. sample of 8,000 adults, found that 72 percent of workplace bullies were superiors who heaped abuse on subordinates. Similarly, 60 percent of workplace incivility is top-down, with bosses subjecting followers to inconsiderate words and deeds. Vile bosses are especially prevalent in particular industries, notably medicine. Researchers tracking 2,884 U.S. medical students found that few survived their training without being belittled by superiors—especially by those doctors who oversee their work with patients: 63 percent were belittled by clinical professors (experienced doctors who serve as teaching faculty) and 71 percent by residents (rookie doctors who supervise medical students most directly). Doctors and other superiors also often treat nurses like dirt—more than 90 percent of nurses report ongoing verbal abuse in some studies.

If there were truth in advertising, many bosses would adopt the motto "Assholes are us." Or they might use what the Urban Dictionary calls the "deadly hybrid of *boss* and *asshole*" and adopt "Bossholes are us," as it is more succinct. Unfortunately, bossholes rarely recognize themselves. As we've seen, bosses are often clueless to how followers interpret their moves. Like other human beings, bosses don't see their own flaws and do fancy themselves as better than the rest. The Zogby survey is again instructive: 37 percent of Americans reported being victims of workplace bullies, but less than 1 percent reported being bullies. This bosshole gap means that even if you realize that most bosses risk becoming insensitive jerks, and your followers agree you are a certified asshole, you probably don't view yourself as widely feared and despised. This gap also means that you likely won't recognize episodes when you've been a temporary bosshole.

This gap is reflected in many stories I've been told since writing *The No Asshole Rule*. Consider the sales manager who completed my twenty-four-item ARSE Test (Asshole Rating Self-Exam) with his vice president in mind. The

ARSE is a nonscientific survey comprising twenty-four cruel and rude moves that assholes make; over two hundred thousand people have completed it online. ARSE items include "Sometimes you just can't contain your contempt toward the jerks and losers in your workplace," "You constantly interrupt people because, after all, what you have to say is more important," and "You find it useful to glare at, insult, and even occasionally holler at some of the idiots at your workplace—otherwise, they never seem to shape up." This manager estimated that his vice president displayed twenty-two of the twenty-four demeaning behaviors, which ranked him as "a full-blown certified asshole." When the manager told this vice president about the ARSE, he completed it online and bragged, "I got a '3'; I am a great boss." This meant the VP rated himself as displaying only three of the twenty-four demeaning behaviors, indicating under the ARSE scoring guide that "you don't sound like a certified asshole, unless you are fooling yourself." The "thoroughly disgusted" manager believed that his VP was, indeed, fooling himself, and he responded by leaving for another job a few weeks later.

This bosshole gap isn't surprising given, as we saw in chapter 1, that bosses—like other human beings—are notoriously poor at evaluating their own performance. The worst bosses ignore or deny any hint they suffer from this gap or other blind spots. The best take seriously how others judge them—and accept the uncomfortable fact that followers' perceptions are often more valid than their own. As we see next, bosses who have enough self-awareness to squelch their inner jerk protect their followers' performance and humanity, and their careers and reputations, too.

The Damage Done

Evidence of the harm inflicted by bossholes is cataloged in books including *The Bully at Work, The Cost of Bad Behavior,* and *The No Asshole Rule,* along with many academic articles. The upshot is that you can't be a great boss if you don't keep your inner jerk in check. The damage to your followers' humanity renders you incompetent in my book. And even if you don't give a hoot about "warm, fuzzy people" stuff, the impaired performance ought to get your attention.

Bossholes make people sick. Their negative impact on physical health is especially well documented in European studies of heart disease. A Finnish study of 804 factory workers showed that those reporting unfair treatment from superiors later suffered higher death rates from heart problems. Similarly, a British study that tracked over 6,000 civil servants for twenty years found that when their bosses criticized them unfairly, didn't listen to their problems, and rarely offered praise, they suffered more angina, heart attacks, and deaths from heart disease. As we saw in chapter 1, a ten-year Swedish study of over 3,000 workers found that those with lousy bosses suffered far more heart attacks. I would call those lousy Swedish bosses incompetent assholes, as they were bad at getting things done and treated people like dirt.

Certified bossholes ruin their followers' mental health, provoking anxiety, depression, and posttraumatic stress syndrome. The study that tracked 2,884 U.S. medical students found that harassed and belittled students were prone to feeling stressed and depressed, to binge drinking, and to thoughts of suicide. The resulting despair pervades interviews with bossholes' victims, who use terms like *maimed, ripped,* and *broken* to describe their feelings. A police officer said it felt like "pulling wings off a fly." Another target called it "Chinese water torture." And a teacher said that eventually she turned emotionally numb, "just like a zombie."

Bullies do collateral damage as well, provoking anxiety, despair, and withdrawal among employees who witness their nastiness. The 2007 Zogby survey suggested that when the impact on victims and witnesses are combined, bullies have driven over 20 million U.S. employees from their jobs. The collateral damage to loved ones is especially disturbing. Professor Pamela Lutgen-Sandvik quotes a wife who couldn't support her bullied husband any longer: "He became invisible to me because I could not stand to look at him like this. Every day he went into a crazy workplace. And every day I wanted to run away."

When I asked people who read my blog if they or their friends and families had suffered collateral damage from asshole bosses, I was inundated with discouraging e-mails and comments. A woman wrote she had just ruined her family dinner because, after being berated, belittled, and micromanaged by her boss all day, she started screaming at her husband and kids. A victim of an "asshole narcissist of a boss" typed out a list of "the ripple effects for me and my family," including: "Once I got home, I had to unload, and every night became a bitch session that my wife had to listen to. It went all through dinner, and generally lasted two hours." Amid the wreckage, though, there is some dark humor and justice. An executive from the southwestern United States wrote about her demeaning and incompetent CEO, noting, "My children nicknamed him Giant Butthole." There was justice because this executive banded together with colleagues and got Mr. Giant Butthole fired. Now she is the CEO and is committed to building a civilized workplace.

Bossholes' wicked shenanigans damage performance in diverse and devastating ways. Their trampled followers are less committed to and satisfied with their jobs. Their targets are also less creative, expend less effort, persist less on difficult tasks, and more prone to be absent and quit. Wayne Hochwarter and Samantha Engelhard's survey of 180 employees found those with abusive bosses were five times more likely (30 percent vs. 6 percent) to admit to slowing down or making errors on purpose. Timothy Judge and his colleagues tracked sixty-four employees for three weeks, gathering detailed information from employees and their supervisors. They found that even model employees turned "negative and unproductive if their bosses are rude or mean spirited," gossiping rather than working, stealing, backstabbing, and taking longer breaks. A study of 265 fast-food restaurants examined abusive general managers (e.g., "tells me my thoughts and feelings are stupid" and "expresses anger at me when he or she is mad for another reason"). These bosshole-led restaurants suffered far higher levels of "food loss," reflecting counterproductive employee responses like stealing and not expending the effort to use ingredients efficiently.

Organizations where bossholes run rampant can suffer ruined reputations. Imagine the effect on customers when George Brunt, general counsel of executive coaching firm Prosper, Inc., told a reporter, "We're not the mean waterboarding company that people think we are."

Why would Brunt issue this bizarre denial?

In early 2008, former Prosper salesperson Chad Hudgens filed a lawsuit alleging he was waterboarded at a company picnic. The *Washington Post* reported (drawing on the lawsuit) that Hudgens's boss, Joshua Christopherson, created a "testosterone-poisoned environment." If his team went a day without making a sale, Christopherson took away their chairs and made them work standing up until they made one. And he allegedly called the hunk of wood on his desk "the two-by-four of motivation." Christopherson apparently outdid himself on May 29, 2007. According to the suit and statements by Prosper's management, the team was in a sales slump, so Christopherson asked for volunteers for a "team-building exercise." Chad Hudgens complied. The *Post* reported, minutes later, "he lay on his back with his head downhill, and coworkers knelt on either side of him, pinning the young sales rep down while their supervisor poured water from a gallon jug over his nose and mouth."

Christopherson reportedly said, "You saw how hard Chad fought for air right there. I want you to go back inside and fight that hard to make sales." Prosper general counsel George Brunt did not dispute that water was poured down Hudgens's throat during the company picnic. But Brunt defended Prosper with claims that the exercise lasted less than twenty seconds, that Christopherson kept asking Hudgens if he was okay, and that "I can't say he wasn't held down, but anybody holding him would have let him up if he'd held his hand up."

The suit alleged that Hudgens suffered from anxiety and depression after the incident and soon left the firm. Prosper management admitted the stunt was unauthorized and misguided, but argued it "[fell] far short of torture." Although the suit was dismissed in August 2008 (on a technicality, not on the factual claims), it was a public relations nightmare for Prosper. This story is extreme, but regardless of how your organization gets a reputation for asshole poisoning, it can alienate customers and employees.

Leaders who calculate the TCA (Total Cost of Assholes) for their organizations are sometimes inspired to be less nasty and to reform or expel abusive bosses. The costs add up quickly—health care, lost productivity, theft, lost creativity, errors, recruiting costs, and public relations expenses, to name a few. As I showed in *The No Asshole Rule*, the costs generated by just one asshole can be staggering: A group of HR managers at a software firm got so ticked off at "Ethan," an abusive star sales manager, that they spent days calculating the costs generated by this creep—expenses like replacing assistants he drove out, anger management training and lawyers, and the extra time managers and executives devoted to calming Ethan and cleaning up his messes. The HR managers calculated the TCA for Ethan for one year was $160,000.

"Asshole taxes" are another cost. People who work for, or with, known assholes often extract extra pay in return for enduring poor treatment. HR executives sometimes provide combat pay for assistants assigned to bossholes— to compensate them for the abuse and persuade them to stay. Numerous lawyers, consultants, and accountants have told me that when a client has treated them badly, they avoid working for them again unless they are desperate, and when they must, they often charge higher rates to make themselves feel better and because assholes consume extra time and emotional energy. A European consultant explained his firm's evidence-based "asshole pricing" in a comment on my blog:

> We've therefore abandoned the old pricing altogether and simply have a list of difficult customers who get charged more. Before *The No Asshole Rule* became widely known, we were calling this Asshole Pricing. It isn't just a tax, a surcharge on the regular price; the entirety of the price quoted is driven by Asshole considerations.

Bossholes also generate legal costs. Lawyers are still arguing over whether it is unlawful to be an "equal opportunity asshole," that is, to treat everyone like dirt regardless of gender, race, age, religion, or national origin. But they smell the money. At least seventeen states are currently considering anti-bullying legislation, and such laws are already on the books in Australia, Canada, England, Ireland, and Sweden. Recent litigation also shows that lawyers can extract handsome cash awards from equal opportunity bossholes. An Indiana lawsuit by perfusionist Joseph E. Doescher (who operated equipment during surgery) claimed he suffered intentional infliction of emotional distress and assault from heart surgeon Dr. Daniel H. Raess—who allegedly screamed and lunged at Doescher and told him that his career was finished. Doescher claimed the resulting severe depression forced him to quit his $100,000-a-year job and take a $20,000-a-year job cleaning dog kennels. A jury awarded $325,000 to Doescher, which was upheld by the Indiana Supreme Court.

Bossholes suffer self-inflicted wounds. As we've seen, bully bosses lead less effective followers—which reflects badly on them, as bosses get so much blame for bad performance. Bossholes also suffer more direct costs. Ethan, the abusive sales manager, was punished with a big reduction in his bonus. Dr. Raess was portrayed as an ogre in the press and the $325,000 judgment was against him, not the hospital. Victims may also band together to get bossholes fired. Pamela Lutgen-Sandvik describes an abusive boss who, ironically, directed a battered women's shelter. This director subjected subordinates to relentless criticism, micromanagement, and personal insults; she was finally sacked after a contingent of seven managers went to a board member's house, aired their complaints, and threatened that if she was not removed, they would quit because, as they said, "We just can't take it anymore."

Causes and Cures for the Common Bosshole

What drives so many bosses to be seen as so cruel by so many followers? I've never met a boss who wants to leave people feeling demeaned, disrespected, and de-energized. Yet many bosses are buffeted by forces that bring out insensitivity and nastiness. As I've said, it is almost as if the job was designed to turn occupants into assholes. It is difficult, arguably impossible, to be a boss (or any human being) without being a temporary asshole now and then. Yet, by being aware of and mindfully battling these forces, bosses can avoid becoming certified assholes and limit the damage done when their inner jerk rears its ugly head.

1. Toxic Tandem and Power Poisoning

Professor Dacher Keltner has studied power dynamics for over fifteen years. He reports, "When researchers give people power in scientific experiments, they are more likely to touch others in potentially inappropriate ways, to flirt in a more direct fashion," to "interrupt others, to speak out of turn, to fail to look at others when they are speaking," and to "tease friends and colleagues in hostile and humiliating fashion." Another of his studies shows that when people get a little power, it dampens how much compassion they convey and how much distress they feel (measured by self-reports and electrocardiograms) when listening to others talk about painful things such as a dying friend or personal failure. Keltner contends, "People with power tend to behave like patients who have damaged their brain's orbitofrontal lobes (the region of the frontal lobes right behind the eye sockets), a condition that seems to cause overly impulsive and insensitive behavior. Thus the experience of power might be thought of as having someone open up your skull and take out that part of your brain so critical to empathy and socially appropriate behavior."

Keltner is a bit overly dramatic here, as there are plenty of empathetic and civilized bosses. But there is strong evidence that power turns people into insensitive jerks who are oblivious to subordinates' needs and actions. There is also convincing evidence that subordinates are hypervigilant about superiors' moves and often assume the worst about their intentions. This toxic tandem means that bosses are often oblivious to the moves they make that piss off and hurt followers. A vice president at an advertising agency told me about a clueless subordinate he reprimanded, an account manager who repeatedly hurled personal insults at his direct reports—telling them their clothes looked terrible or what they ate made them fat, and teasing them about their laziness and limited career options. The vice president's negative feedback came as a complete shock to this manager. He admitted to a lot of "friendly banter," but argued his people loved the teasing and loved him—even though the total opposite was true.

There are other times when the toxic tandem causes bosses to become so self-absorbed that they treat underlings as if they are invisible. In the preface, I described a legal secretary who suffered in silence as attorneys held loud conversations at her desk, interfering with her concentration and hurting her feelings because they acted as if she didn't exist. Similar insensitivity was captured by another legal secretary on her blog, which is entitled She's Lump:

> For a little over a week, I've been making a list of things I hear the many attorneys I work with say on the elevator ride up to my office. It's not as if I'm eavesdropping because I *am* in an elevator after all, and it's somewhat hard to have a conversation without someone taking note—and that someone is obviously ME. These attorneys want to know everyone's business as well as flaunt their own for the whole elevator audience to hear (OK, not all of them are like this). Or maybe they're just fucking loud. Loudly trying to ONE UP the other. One uppers are assholes.

These one-uppers bragged about gold-plated golf clubs, paying massive property taxes, and "how they have their secretaries send their files to them during their weekend trips to their beach houses in Florida or condos in NYC and Vegas." Lump's post ends with an exchange she heard between two attorneys:

> "I bought a new fully loaded Porsche 911 Carrera 4S last night, metallic black with dark gray leather interior. It is NIIIIIIICCCCCE."
>
> "Oh yeah? A few weeks ago I purchased my first AIRPLANE."

When I talk with bosses about power poisoning, they often see it in others, but rarely in themselves. Many of these bosses are deluding themselves—after all, the toxic tandem plagues people in power independently of their personalities. In contrast, the best bosses accept the uncomfortable truth, that "assholes are us," and guard against acting like temporary assholes and developing reputations as certified assholes. This means that as a boss, you need trusted advisors, mentors, and followers who feel safe telling you when you've been a schmuck. A Silicon Valley software firm, SuccessFactors, generated a lot of publicity a few years ago with their "no assholes" policy. Employee Max Goldman explained on the company blog how it worked:

> My own personal experience with no assholes is very simple. Once, my boss was being a jerk. I told him so—in those words. Instead of getting mad, he accepted the comment and we moved on. Later, he thanked me for telling him. My boss thanked me for

calling him a jerk. Let me repeat that. **My boss thanked me for calling him a jerk.** Calling the spade a spade helped everyone work better together and get more done. Can you do that at your company?

Bosses who successfully enlist others to help them avoid and reverse power poisoning usually have a history of treating people with respect, and listening to and learning from criticism rather than getting defensive and shooting the messengers. If you are a boss, urging colleagues and employees to deliver bad news isn't enough; you need to react with grace and try to change when they call you a jerk, like Max Goldman's boss did.

2. Extreme Performance Pressure

Although all bosses risk focusing on performance too much and humanity too little, this balance gets especially out of whack when performance pressure becomes intense—a feature of countless bosses' jobs. Many work in extremely competitive industries and face one tight deadline after another. Most bosses are praised, feel proud, and enjoy handsome incentives when their teams and organizations succeed—and many are blamed, feel shame, lose income, and sometimes are canned when their followers fail. Pressures like these may explain what happened at Prosper, where supervisor Joshua Christopherson apparently poured water down salesperson Chad Hudgens's throat. Even Hudgens reported that Christopherson was upbeat and well-liked by everyone at Prosper. But the performance "pressure-cooker," as Hudgens called it, may have driven his well-liked boss to focus on making sales and to forget about his people's dignity and well-being.

Time pressure causes people to become especially insensitive to others. Surveys by Christine Pearson and Christine Porath reveal that almost 50 percent of workers claim they don't have enough time to be civil on their jobs. A classic experiment demonstrates—with splendid irony—how time pressure undermines sensitivity and humanity. In 1973, psychologists John Darley and Daniel Batson recruited students at the Princeton Theological Seminary to give a brief talk on the Good Samaritan, from a parable in the New Testament about the virtues of helping those in need. After getting their assignment, the seminary students walked outside through an alley to get to the building where their talk was scheduled. In the alley, they encountered a person (a shill planted by the researchers) sitting slumped with his head down and eyes shut, who was coughing and groaning. To top it off, it was freezing (never above 5 degrees Fahrenheit), as the research was done during an unusually cold December in New Jersey. The researchers told some of the seminary students they didn't need to hurry, some to hurry a bit, and some to rush over immediately because they were already late. These differences in time pressure had a huge impact: 63 percent of those in no hurry stopped to help, 45 percent in a bit of a hurry helped, and only 10 percent of those in a big hurry helped—passing just inches from someone apparently in dire need as they rushed to talk about the virtues of Good Samaritans.

John Darley and Daniel Batson attribute such insensitivity to heightened emotional arousal and cognitive narrowing: Freaking out about time pressure causes people to focus on the task at hand and tune out everything else. To battle such narrowing (and the associated grumpiness) when the pressure is on, keep reminding yourself and others of the big picture, to take a long-term time perspective. Some bosses encourage their most sensible and calm people to remind the team when they start losing perspective, bickering, or otherwise taking themselves too seriously. A producer who led a team of computer game designers explained to me how one of his designers earned the nickname Mr. Calm. It happened at a meeting where the producer was hollering at his team because a project was behind schedule and executives were pressing him to move faster. Mr. Calm gently responded to his boss's hysteria with words like "We've all been in this position before, and taking it out on each other just makes things worse" and "We will design a better game if we work deliberately rather than freaking out and doing sloppy things."

The most creative method I've ever heard for calming people anxious about performance pressures was used by an Italian boss whom I met at a Stanford executive program. After a round of performance evaluations where his direct reports seemed overwrought by even minor criticisms, this imaginative boss put things in perspective by taking his charges to a hospice, where they met dying patients and their families. He reminded them that their performance evaluations really don't mean much in the larger scheme of things and then did their next evaluations, right there in the hospice.

Finally, follow David Kelley's advice in chapter 1: If you are a boss with a history of treating followers with dignity and have built up a lot of "love points," your people will probably forgive you if you get nasty now and then when you are under the gun. After all, you have points to burn. But if you are a known asshole, don't expect much sympathy—or extra effort—from followers when the shit hits the fan.

3. Sleep Deprivation, Heat, and Other Bodily Sources of Bad Moods

In early 2002, I spent a delightful day in London promoting my book *Weird Ideas That Work*. The highlight was a radio show on the BBC with the late Sir Peter Parker, an executive widely admired in England for his accomplishments in the private and public sectors—especially for making the trains run on time when he led British Rail. The charming Sir Peter gave many bits of good management advice. My favorite was to take an afternoon nap, which he claimed helped him maintain wisdom and civility throughout his career. Naps are apparently a tradition among British leaders. Winston Churchill, who led the United Kingdom during World War II, praised them, too: "Nature had not intended mankind to work from 8 in the morning until midnight without the refreshment of blessed oblivion which, even if it only lasts 20 minutes, is sufficient to renew all the vital forces."

Research on sleep deprivation shows that Parker and Churchill were onto something, as a lack of sleep causes people to make lousy decisions and turns them into impatient jerks—and when deprivation is severe, people turn irrational and fly into wild rages. Naps dampen such negative effects and also help people who are not sleep deprived to be more effective and civilized. A fifteen- to sixty-minute nap bolsters creativity, alertness, error detection, and mood—even for people who don't usually nap. Sleep researcher Mark Rosekind reports that when he worked at NASA, they gave pilots planned naps in the cockpit: "While two pilots flew the plane, the third would have 40 minutes to nap. We found they would sleep for [an average of] 26 minutes, which boosted their performance by 34% and their alertness by 54%."

So, grab a short snooze and suggest others do, too, especially when it isn't feasible to get a good night's sleep. It will increase your performance and make you a more civilized human being. Successful serial entrepreneur Brian Wiegand, the CEO of Alice.com, is a big fan of naps. He tries to take one each day and encourages his employees to do the same. Wiegand places a rubber band on his door knob as a "do not disturb" signal during nap time. He rejects complaints that naps are unnecessary and unprofessional, pointing to the research and to famous nappers like Albert Einstein, Thomas Edison, John F. Kennedy, and Ronald Reagan.

There are many other physical causes of bad moods, including eating poorly, working excessive hours, long commutes, lack of exercise, and substance abuse. Every boss knows that such problems can turn people into incompetent jerks. But another well-documented source of nastiness gets less attention. As Shakespeare wrote in *Romeo and Juliet*:

I pray thee, good Mercutio, let's retire;
The day is hot, the Capulets abroad,
And, if we meet, we shall not 'scape a brawl,
For now, these hot days, is the mad blood stirring.

Shakespeare got it right. When people are physically hot, they turn mean. Folk sayings like *hot under the collar* and *steamed* are bolstered by research on temperature and aggression: Countries with hot climates suffer higher murder rates and more political violence; more violent crimes occur in hot years; drivers honk at other drivers more on hot than on cold days (especially when their cars don't have air conditioning); research subjects deliver bigger electric shocks to "learners" they are "punishing" when working in hot rooms; people in hot rooms are also less attracted to both friends and strangers; and major-league baseball pitchers apparently turn mean when they are hot under the collar. A study called "Temper and Temperature on the Diamond" by researcher Alan Reifman and his colleagues examined 826 games played during three major-league baseball seasons. These data showed that pitchers were three times more likely to intentionally hit batters (with the baseball) when temperatures were above 90 degrees Fahrenheit compared to when it was below 80 degrees.

There are several theories about why heat makes people grouchy, ranging from arguments that when men sweat it increases testosterone levels (making them more aggressive) to the simple assertion that heat is uncomfortable, which makes people grumpy and thus see things (and other people) in a more negative light. Whatever the reason, keeping yourself and your people cool will help keep life from turning nasty. Beware that when people are already in bad moods, heat magnifies crankiness and aggression. So when you or your followers are already turning mean, take extra care to avoid overheated rooms in winter and meet in nice air-conditioned places, or cool shady spots, in summer.

4. Nasty Role Models

When aspiring bosses are mentored or overseen by people who treat them and others like dirt—whether the aspiring bosses realize it or not—their natural response is to imitate these demeaning ways once they become bosses themselves. Aspiring bosses may also admire and mimic famous (allegedly) nasty bosses such as former Disney CEO Michael Eisner, Academy Award–winning producer Scott Rudin, or lifestyle expert Martha Stewart. As author Scott Berkun suggests, one reason bosses become assholes is "in trying to emulate someone more powerful than themselves, they didn't separate the good qualities from the bad and copied it all."

The ubiquity of bad role models helps explain why, among physicians, assholes seem to breed like rabbits. A head surgeon at a large hospital wrote on my blog:

> I trained at an "elite" training program at an Ivy League hospital....I witnessed episodes of unbelievable mental cruelty on a daily basis. As residents, we met every Friday for a few beers at a local bar after another arduous work week. We kept a leather-bound journal book. The highlight of the happy hour was nominating and electing the "Attending Asshole of the Week" or "AAOTW." Each aggrieved individual would recount their episode with an attending that would merit their nomination as the "Asshole of the Week." The group voted and the "winner's" name was entered into the journal book. A brief synopsis of the "asshole incident" was also placed in the journal.

It is difficult for any person to avoid imitating teachers and authority figures. When everyone around you acts like a jerk and admires the creeps in charge, there is no good behavior to copy, and refraining from nastiness is often treated as a weakness. Yet when aspiring bosses band together to create countervailing social pressure against imitating demeaning mentors, they can avoid following in their vile footsteps. This is exactly what those young doctors at the Ivy League school did. The (now) head surgeon explained:

> This was twenty years ago. It is possible to look at these sessions as "bitch" sessions with no meaningful result. However, every one of my resident colleagues learned from those sessions. We learned how destructive "asshole" behavior was in our specialty. We vowed not to imitate the pathologic behavior we encountered daily. Twenty years later, we are now the program chairs and department chairmen. We are spread across the country. I am proud to say that everybody who was a part of that Friday group runs their training programs with an unwritten "no asshole" rule.

When the top dog can remain calm and civilized—even when the pressure is on and the chips are down—this antidote to asshole poisoning rolls down the hierarchy as bosses and others follow suit.

5. Asshole-Infested Workplaces

Even bosses who aren't bred or led by assholes turn mean when they are knee-deep in demeaning colleagues and customers. Emotions are remarkably contagious. When people are surrounded by jerks, they usually mimic such behavior and don't realize they are doing so. When my students get job offers, I suggest they take a good look at how their future colleagues treat each other—because that is probably how they will act if they take the job. I add that their chances of catching the disease is also high if the job entails lots of contact with asshole customers and clients. To illustrate, a pastor in a small Southern church wrote me that her board of directors and most parishioners treated her (and each other) with contempt. She admitted, "I entered a toxic environment and I too have fallen for being an asshole (actually I call them the 'adult cooties'). I am trying to turn around and be more sensitive, especially as I tend to stress my secretary rather than kick my dog."

There are also places where treating colleagues with disrespect and contempt is so ingrained that bosses who don't return fire are crushed like bugs. The best bosses in these hellholes treat followers well, but heap strategic abuse on other bosses and other teams to protect their people's jobs, resources, and sanity. One of the most popular postings on my blog was "Marge's Asshole Management Metric." This is a true story about a manager named Marge who rated employees on a four-point scale, ranging from 0 ("a very nice person, and very passive"), to 1 ("a normal person who can occasionally assert yourself on an issue you are passionate about"), to 2 ("consistently assert yourself in a non-confrontational way and are occasionally an asshole, but you feel horrible about it afterwards"), to 3 ("can consistently be an asshole and you either do not recognize this or you simply enjoy it"). As I learned from Marge and a guy named Bill who worked for her in two companies, Marge taught this system to her direct reports, including hand signals she used during meetings to communicate when they needed to increase or decrease their assholeness. Marge explained:

> The system originated at another Silicon Valley company that had a far more confrontational and abrasive culture. Political survival demanded that people be consistently a 2.0 and sometimes a 2.5. I had a number of 0.5s on my team and we were all concerned that we were getting battered and beaten by teams that consisted of 3.0s.

Fortunately, by the time I heard this story, Marge and Bill moved to a civilized company, so Marge's people rarely needed to crank-up their venom beyond a 1.

If you are a boss in an asshole-infested organization, or in a nasty neighborhood of an otherwise civilized workplace, the best solution is to escape—like Marge and Bill did. But if you are trapped in a nasty place (at least for now), you can take steps to protect yourself and your people. First, have as little contact with local assholes as you can. Nastiness is remarkably infectious, so the less you are exposed the less nasty you will get, the less you will need to fight back, and the less your mental and physical health will suffer. Second, as I suggested to bosses stuck overseeing rotten apples, learn the fine art of emotional detachment and indifference—don't let their poison touch your soul. A project manager at a biotech company explained to me during a dinner party:

If assholes could fly, this place would be an airport. I've kept my sanity by only going to the meetings that I can't avoid and talking to my three bosses only when absolutely necessary. I just go through the motions around these people. Sometimes I pretend it isn't me, that I am watching some other guy deal with the assholes. The secret to my success is that I've learned not to give a shit.

There are plenty of times in life when feeling passionate and having strong emotional reactions to others promotes performance and humanity. But when you face an onslaught of mean-spirited creeps, practicing the art of indifference can protect your followers and loved ones from the ugliest part of yourself.

Finally, if you are trapped in a place where assholes rule the roost, the more you as a boss can do to create asshole-free zones for your direct reports, the more your people will be exposed to and spread civility rather than contempt. A former U.S. Army officer wrote me that most of his superiors were certified assholes who kept rewarding and promoting jerks just like them. But his battalion commander was a countervailing force, "the polar opposite of an asshole" and "probably the most professional military officer I've ever met in my life":

> I got out of line a few times and he brought me in immediately and counseled me on my behavior. He didn't yell or belittle me, but I got the point and was

embarrassed that I had let him down. I'm a better person for it and I'd like to think that I have picked up his habits and that I emulate his actions by treating people the way they should be treated.

Looking Back, Will You Be Proud or Embarrassed?

Regardless of why it happens, bosses who treat their people like dirt usually do more harm than good, even when they act with the best of intentions. Most people don't want to be known as assholes, don't want to think of themselves as assholes, and are ashamed when others give them feedback that they are demeaning creeps. That is why this chapter dug into the causes of and cures for the common bosshole, which are summarized (and extended a bit) in the accompanying list of "Bosshole Busters."

After spending several years immersed in the "asshole problem" and contemplating cures for bossholes here, I realized there is a central theme implied in much of what I say and write, but I rarely spell out: *Embarrassment and pride are perhaps the most powerful antidotes to asshole poisoning.* Consider this pair of diagnostic questions. If you are a boss, ask yourself: When you look back at how you've treated followers, peers, and superiors, *in their eyes*, will you have earned the right to be proud of yourself? Or will *they believe* that you ought to be ashamed of yourself and embarrassed by how you have trampled on others' dignity day after day? I believe that, even more so than financial rewards, most human beings are motivated to avoid embarrassment and feel pride. By keeping a firm focus on these two questions, bosses can avoid the asshole poisoning suffered by too many other superiors who wield power over followers.

The power of pride and shame was brought home to me a few years back as I was waiting in line at a UPS store near the Stanford campus. I started talking with another customer, an intense and friendly guy in his sixties who had a lot to say but never offered his name. After he learned about my work, he described how, early in his career, he earned a well-deserved reputation as a bosshole. The cure, he said, came when one of his direct reports asked for a transfer to another team. When he asked why, this fellow told him that he couldn't take the hollering, insults, and cruel taunts any longer, and he hated being on a team where good people fled as soon as they could. Then he suggested, "Perhaps you should imagine that your fourteen-year-old son is following you around all day, and whenever you deal with one of us ask yourself: *Would my son be proud or ashamed of how I am treating this person?*" From that moment on, the man told me, he began imagining that his son was judging his every move at work—which proved to be an enormously useful mind game for keeping his nastiness in check and inspiring him to treat others with kindness and dignity throughout the rest of his career.

BOSSHOLE BUSTERS
Tips for Squelching Your Inner Jerk

1. If you are a boss, assume the motto "Assholes are us" means you, too, not just the other schmucks.
2. Post a bosshole bounty: pay twenty dollars to anyone who tells you when you have been a jerk.
3. Assign confident and sensible followers to be your bosshole monitors. Link their performance evaluation and pay to telling you when you've blown it and helping you contain your inner jerk.
4. When you realize you've treated people like dirt, apologize to them and acknowledge to witnesses that such nastiness is unacceptable.
5. If you are a certified asshole, or a recovering one, team up with a "toxic handler," someone more patient and better liked to coach you and clean up your messes.
6. If your boss is a flaming asshole, you will probably catch the disease. Escape as fast as you can or, failing that, spend as little time around the creep as possible.
7. If clients treat you like dirt, fire them if possible. If you can't, charge asshole taxes, give employees who work with them combat pay, and limit everyone's exposure to these creeps.
8. Squelch your inner jerk by practicing indifference and emotional detachment when you get angry, focus on performance too much and humanity too little, or are knee-deep in a pack of assholes.
9. If you or your charges have been acting like assholes

lately, make sure to hold meetings in a nice cool place.

10. Watch the e-mail. Remember how easy it is to spew out angry and insensitive words, or unwittingly hurt others' feelings when using this emotionally thin medium.

11. Imagine it is ten years from now and you are looking back at how you've treated others. Do you think—in your followers' eyes—that you will have earned the right to be proud of yourself? Or do your people believe that when you look back, you will deserve to be ashamed of yourself?

SECTION III

The Upshot

CHAPTER 9

It's All About You

Last year, I led a workshop at Stanford on being a good boss during tough times. As we walked to lunch afterward, a manager from the session told me about a vice president at his company—one of his bosses. A few weeks earlier, a secretary in his office walked up to this vice president and asked, "When are the layoffs coming?" The boss was flabbergasted. He had no clue how she discovered big cuts were in the offing: The decision had just been made and extreme care had been taken to keep it under wraps. When the bewildered VP asked how she knew, the secretary answered that when bad news was coming, he couldn't bring himself to look his people in the eye. This VP had what poker players call a tell, a habit or quirk that revealed when he was hiding something (bad news in this case). The codeword among his charges was "The boss is wearing interesting shoes today."

The "interesting shoes" story reflects a pervasive theme

in *Good Boss, Bad Boss*, one that weaves together many stories and studies here and distinguishes the best from the worst bosses: If you are a boss, your success depends on staying in tune with how others think, feel, and react to you. Bosses who persistently promote performance and humanity devote considerable energy to reading and responding to followers' feelings and actions, and those of other key players like superiors, peers, and customers. Of course, there is no single magical or simple thing that defines a great boss. As I emphasized at the outset, anyone who promises you an easy or instant pathway to success is either ignorant or dishonest—or both. The moves that great bosses make are too complex, varied, messy, and unpredictable to be captured by any single theme, slogan, or set of steps.

Yet some skills and aspirations are more important than others. Developing and sustaining self-awareness ought to be at the top of the list for every boss. David Dunning, of Cornell University, shows that a hallmark of poor performers is a lack of self-awareness; they consistently overestimate their skills in just about any task that requires intellectual and social skills, such as debating, having a sense of humor, or interviewing others. In contrast, Dunning finds that self-awareness is a hallmark of the best performers—they are especially cognizant of their strengths and weaknesses, and fret about overcoming pitfalls that can undermine their performance. When it comes to bosses, the best might laugh at the VP in the "interesting shoes" story. But they are painfully aware that they could easily be that guy—that every boss is prone to bouts of cluelessness and to forgetting how closely followers track every little thing they do. The best bosses reduce the risk of self-delusion by seeking and responding to hints and hard data about how others read their moods and moves. They urge followers to challenge them with enlightening— and disconcerting—questions, like when the VP's secretary asked, "When are the layoffs coming?" They want their followers (and bosses, peers, and customers, too) to keep feeding them such information, no matter how unpleasant and unflattering, because they are obsessed with how their words and deeds are interpreted by others.

The upshot is, to be a great boss you've got to think and act as if it is all about you. Your success depends on being fixated on yourself. On the surface, this conclusion clashes with advice from many gurus and experts. Former GE CEO Jack Welch and Stanford's Robert Joss (dean of the Graduate School of Business for a decade), for example, implore managers, "It's not about you." I agree with the spirit of this advice, as the aim is to discourage bosses from falling prey to their most selfish and destructive instincts. Yet I question the words because most bosses, like most human beings, are remarkably self-obsessed—and that isn't necessarily a bad thing. Yes, the worst are selfish, oblivious to their charges, and cling to dangerous delusions about their magnificent leadership skills. The best are equally self-obsessed but have different motivations. Their obsession isn't for egotistical or for selfish reasons. On the contrary, they focus on controlling their moods and moves, accurately interpreting their impact on others, and making adjustments on the fly because they want their people to produce work that others will admire—and to feel respect and dignity along the way.

As we saw in chapter 1, Linda Hudson learned the importance of self-awareness when she became the first female president of General Dynamics and, after her first day on the job, a dozen women in her office began imitating how she tied her scarf. Hudson then realized, "It really was now about me and the context of setting the tone for the organization. That was a lesson I have never forgotten—that as a leader, people are looking at you in a way that you could not have imagined in other roles." Such scrutiny and the responsibility that goes with it is, Hudson added, "something that I think about virtually every day."

Intel executive Patricia "Pat" McDonald demonstrated similar awareness in 2006 when managing a factory in Hillsboro, Oregon. As part of a company-wide reduction, several managers at the plant lost jobs. An engineer who worked for Pat, Sumit Guha, told me how "she recounted the contributions of these employees in an open forum, wishing them luck, acknowledging that these employees were being let go for no fault of their own, and we all gave these employees a hand in appreciation of their contributions."

Things got worse in early 2009 when Intel announced the factory would cease production at year's end because it was using older technology—and approximately one thousand workers would lose their positions. Pat not only expressed concern and compassion, she took a stance that demonstrated she had her employees' backs. Pat quickly announced to her team that although output metrics would continue to be important, helping people get through the transition was a higher priority—especially finding affected employees new jobs inside and outside of Intel. Pat and her team not only provided extensive outplacement counseling and related services, they personally visited numerous local employers to campaign for new jobs for their people. Managers and employees emulated this behavior. For example, employees shared job search leads and helped each other prepare for interviews, even as they were vying for the same positions.

Sumit emphasized that Pat's dogged efforts to "earn trust and respect from a process of engagement" and her ability to understand "the implications of decisions from the employees' point of view and adjust her course of action accordingly" were what separated her from ordinary bosses. This "deep sense of benevolent care" was especially constructive after the end of production was announced because, "at a time when the economy was collapsing, her actions helped maintain a sense of calm amongst us." Pat's emphasis on people and connection with them not only instilled calm, her priorities helped many find good new jobs. And plant performance didn't suffer a bit; productivity, efficiency, and quality reached record levels in 2009.

Pat's people admired her because she was in tune with what it felt like to be them, and she focused on how the things she said and did shaped their moods, efforts, and loyalty—whether they lost jobs or remained at Intel. Pat's words and deeds and their impact on followers like Sumit—in concert with many of the stories, studies, and advice in *Good Boss, Bad Boss*—suggest two questions that every boss ought to fret over and focus on each day. To steal a phrase from Sumit, these are two "acid tests" for great bosses.

The first acid test is whether people want to work for the boss and would enthusiastically choose to do so again. Recall from chapter 4 how Oakland Police Sergeant John Ludden was so widely respected that several veteran officers chose the unpopular graveyard shift just so they could work with Ludden, rather than a more desirable day or evening shift with another sergeant. In the same spirit, Sumit (who now has another job at Intel) told me that Pat meets his acid test for a great boss: "Would you want to work for her again?" This is a damn good test for any boss.

The second acid test stems from the upshot of this chapter—the best bosses, like Pat McDonald, are hypersensitive to how others feel about them and the work their people do. They keep fretting over and searching for clues to questions like: What strikes my people most about my moves and moods? How do they feel about my competence and compassion? How do they react to the big and little things I do? If forced to pick the most crucial question among the many raised in *Good Boss, Bad Boss*, I would ask: "Are you in tune with what it feels like to work for you?"

I wonder, dear bosses, what would your people say about you? Would they say that you live in a fool's paradise, where every day is an "interesting shoes" day for you? Or would they say that you are in tune with how it feels to be them and work for you?

Your Stories and Ideas About Bosses

Dear Reader,

The ideas in *Good Boss, Bad Boss* are heavily influenced by the stories, suggestions, and evidence people have given me about what the best (and worst) bosses do. I also have learned much from the thoughtful questions that people have asked me in person and online about how they can become a better boss, help their boss succeed, or battle back against a crummy boss. I pride myself in giving personal answers to everyone who writes me, as I am grateful when people take time to share their experiences and ideas. I'd love to keep this exchange of ideas going. If you would like to send me an e-mail about your experiences being a boss, dealing with a boss, or anything else provoked by the ideas in this book, please visit my blog Work Matters at www.bobsutton.net and just click on "E-mail me" in the upper-left-hand corner. You can also read and comment on stories and research about bosses and other workplace issues in my blog. Please note that by sending me your story, you are giving me permission to use it in the things I write and say. But I promise not to use your name unless you give me permission.

Thank you. I look forward to hearing from you about what it takes to become—and remain—a great boss.

Robert Sutton
Stanford University

ACKNOWLEDGMENTS

The journey required to imagine and write *Good Boss, Bad Boss* has been full of twists and turns. As the preface reveals, this book was inspired by responses to *The No Asshole Rule*. I realized that the lion's share of the stories people were telling me centered on working for a boss or being a boss. The "asshole problem" was a part (albeit an emotionally hot one) of a broader concern about the differences between good bosses and bad bosses, and a desire to understand the mindsets and moves of the best bosses. As I began writing this book, I realized that this was a topic I had been working on and fretting over for decades. I admire people who write about grand organizational strategies and broad economic trends. But I've always been most comfortable and engaged when studying the nitty-gritty of organizational life, the little moments of joy and pain, what it feels like to wield power over others, how people react to leaders, and all that other "human" stuff.

This enduring interest means that *Good Boss, Bad Boss* isn't just a product of the fifteen months or so I spent trying to type out and improve the sentences here and—often—deleting them and trying some new ones. It means that I've been working on this book my whole professional life, and even before that, when I listened to my mother and father complain about (and occasionally praise) their bosses. And when my dad became a boss, I saw and heard about his frustrations and accomplishments. I am tempted to thank the thousands of people who have shaped how I think about and judge the differences between the best and worst bosses. I have restrained myself, but please forgive me if these acknowledgments run a bit long. I put them in the back of the book because they are easier to skip that way. But I never would have accomplished anything without the people mentioned below, and so many others.

For starters, I want to thank my colleagues at Stanford for their ideas and support, and for putting up with my sometimes strange behavior. Jeff Pfeffer has had an especially large impact on me. Jeff is my closest friend at Stanford and a delight to disagree with; I have learned more from writing with and arguing with Jeff than anyone else. His influence is evident throughout this book. In particular, the ideas here are shaped by two books we wrote together, *The Knowing-Doing Gap* and *Hard Facts, Dangerous Half-Truths, and Total Nonsense.* In recent years, I've had the privilege of working with, listening to, and drinking some lovely wine with Hayagreeva "Huggy" Rao. Huggy provided offbeat ideas, brilliant leads, and common sense—and listened to my whining now and then—as I've written this book. Huggy has the burden of being the wisest person I know at Stanford, so I often turn to him for advice. Chip Heath, also at the Stanford Business School, provided bursts of brilliance (and useful critiques) at key junctures, notably in helping me pick a title for the book. I also appreciate all the support and ideas I've received from Diane Bailey, Steve Barley, and Pam Hinds at the Center for Work, Technology and Organization, and from Tom Byers and Tina Seelig at the Stanford Technology Ventures Program. I've also learned massive amounts from past and current Stanford doctoral students including Yosem Companys, Ralph Maurer, Liz Gerber, and Isaac Waisberg.

I've had the privilege of teaching with a host of experienced and thoughtful bosses at Stanford's Hasso Plattner Institute of Design—which everyone calls "the d.school." They've taught me much about what it is like to be a boss and work for one. The d.school was founded by David Kelley, who, in addition to being a Stanford professor, was the CEO (and is now chairman) of IDEO—arguably the most renowned innovation firm in the world. David's wisdom pervades this book, and not just in those places where I mention his name. I also have learned a huge amount from teaching and talking with Michael Dearing, Diego Rodriguez, Perry Klebahn, Webb McKinney, and

Kris Woyzbun. I want to give special thanks to Debra Dunn, who has been involved as a coach or co-teacher in nearly every d.school class I have ever taught. Debra constantly enlightens me about the difference between good and bad bosses; she held diverse management positions during the years she was at HP, from leading small teams, to being a general manager of a big business, to being an executive vice president in charge of strategy. And now, besides teaching at the d.school and being on several nonprofit boards, Debra is mentoring the management team at start-ups including Cooliris. It is a privilege to work with such thoughtful people, as they all have spent years dealing with the challenges that I study, talk, and write about, and they are always quick to point out when my academic theories are misguided or useless fantasies.

I had able research assistance from two Stanford undergraduates, Eliza Wiraatmadja and Randy Yang. Daphne Chang and Paul Reist at Stanford's Graduate School of Business library helped in numerous key ways, and I am most grateful to them. I thank Tim Keely for helping me with some pretty weird technology problems. I thank my assistant, Roz Morf, who helps me with many chores—especially dealing with the sometimes bewildering nuances of the Stanford bureaucracy. I want to give especially strong acknowledgment and thanks to James Plummer, my dean at the Stanford Engineering School. Without Jim's steady support and compassion, it would have been mighty difficult for me to get through the last five or six years of my life. I am lucky to have a caring and unselfish boss like Jim, and I appreciate it.

I thank all the people who have told me so many diverse, disturbing, and inspiring workplace stories, many of which appear in *Good Boss, Bad Boss*. Hundreds of people have sent me stories about working for or being a boss in response to posts on my blog Work Matters. There are many of you that I can't thank by name because you have asked me to protect your confidentiality; I always respect such wishes, but know you have my gratitude. I do have permission to use the names of some of these folks, so I want to give a big thanks to Bob Bennett, Matthew May, and Margie Mauldin. For providing stories for this book and helping in other ways, I also thank my fellow bloggers, including Scott Berkun, Kelley Eskridge, CV Harquail, Guy Kawasaki, Dave Livingston, Maureen Rogers, Gretchen Rubin, Todd Sattersten, Pamela Slim, and the anonymous legal secretary who writes the blog She's Lump. I thank all the people who have told me many of the other stories here and been patient with me as I asked for fact-checking and corrections. These include Corey Billington, Brad Bird, Wally Bock, Matt Brownfield, Rudy Crespo, Rob Cross, David Darragh, Leslie Dixon, Sumit Guha, Bill George, Michael Giuliano, Nick Gottuso, John Hennessy, Chuck House, Claudia Kotchka, John Lilly, Lisa Maulhardt, Bill Mackenzie, Patricia McDonald, Joe Mello, Lenny Mendonca, Andy Papathanassiou, Joel Podolny, Paul Purcell, Bernie Roth, Ann Rhoades, Margaret Rowland,

Marie-Pierre Vaslet, and the inspiring Bonny Warner-Simi. I want to give special thanks to Randy Komisar, who not only provided many details about Bill Campbell's inspiring leadership at GO, he answered every question that I asked him with remarkably thoughtful and eloquent text.

Several others helped develop this book in important ways. Julia Kirby, my longtime editor at *Harvard Business Review*, did an inspired job working over and improving the 2009 *HBR* article "How to Be a Good Boss in a Bad Economy," where I developed several core ideas for chapter 7. Marc Hershon, who among many other things is coauthor of *Why I Hate People* and invented the names of many modern products, including BlackBerry and Swiffer, spent hours talking with me and brainstorming different titles. Marc, sorry that "Top Dog on a Tightrope" didn't quite fit, but I still love it and will use that title for something some day. And special thanks to Hollis Heimbouch for providing inspiration and therapy at several crucial junctures.

I also want to give the strongest possible thanks to Catherine Casalino, Susan Kare, Heidi Nilsen, and Anne Twomey. These four people demonstrated rare patience, persistence, attention to detail, and tolerance for my picky feedback during the prolonged—and I believe ultimately successful—process of designing the cover. I think of each of these four women as traveling through life with a halo over her head—each was an angel at every stage despite my sometimes devilish moves. I also thank Mark DeWys, Brad Doan, and Gale Moutrey from Steelcase who went above and beyond the call of duty to provide us with the great picture of the Leap chair on the cover.

I am mighty lucky to work with two of the best literary agents in the business, the wise and deeply experienced Don Lamm, who has been in my corner and ready to do everything from suggesting topics for books, to arguing for big changes in my manuscripts, to editing sentences, to badgering bookstores for not carrying my books, to buying me dinner ever since we started working together four books ago. I am equally lucky to work with Christy Fletcher, who has used her common sense and grit to help me in a hundred ways. One of those ways was to make sure that I could work with Rick Wolff from Business Plus again. Rick was my editor for *The No Asshole Rule*. I constantly appreciated his ability to understand my strengths and flaws, put up with my quirks and moods, and gently—and oh so skillfully—keep me focused on making *Good Boss, Bad Boss* a little more useful, a little more fun, and a little more clear each day during the many months I worked on the manuscript. One of the best parts of working with Rick and Business Plus was that Kallie Shimek took charge of the copyediting again. Kallie is such a master of her craft that one of my favorite parts of finishing the book was answering the wise questions

Kallie raised and marveling at the hundreds of small changes that made me sound smarter and more coherent than I really am.

I thank my loving and often wacky family for their support and patience. My mother, Annette Sutton, has encouraged me at every turn and understood my long periods of isolation as I have pounded out this book. My children, Tyler, Claire, and Eve, have joined the brainstorming about ideas here and—drawing especially on their experiences with teachers, coaches, and school administrators—have expressed strong ideas about the differences between good and bad bosses. Tyler despises petty tyrants. Claire can't stand teachers, coaches, or fellow camp counselors who are lazy. And Eve, who especially dislikes selfish authority figures, cracked me up one day when she proposed that one clueless egomaniac who was oppressing her and her friends "needs to go sit in a room and not come out until she realizes that the world does not revolve around her."

Finally, I am most grateful to my wife, Marina Park, who inspires me and keeps me grounded in reality. Marina has been a boss for a long time, first at a large law firm for many years and now as CEO of the Northern California Girl Scouts. Marina read the entire manuscript and made dozens of suggestions that made the book better. Even more important than that, by being with Marina I see how much she cares about and gives of herself to the people she works with and the fifty thousand or so girls they serve—and especially how hard she works to stay in tune with what her staff, volunteers, and those girls need to succeed and feel proud of their accomplishments. I dedicate this book to Marina.

NOTES

Preface

2 **I talked with a Hollywood insider:** Rudin's antics are summarized in Kate Kelly and Merissa Marr, "Boss-Zilla!" *Wall Street Journal*, September 24, 2005, http://online.wsj. com/article_email/SB112749746571150033-IJjfYNglaB4n52naXqIb6qFm4.html (accessed August 11, 2009). A variation of the "possibly mythical" story about Rudin firing an assistant and dumping him on a Los Angeles freeway is reported in a book by a screenwriter who worked with Rudin. See Paul Rudnick, *I Shudder* (New York: Harper, 2009), 112. Rudnick reports that despite Rudin's tantrums, outrageous demands, and impatience, deep down he is a thoughtful and generous person.

3 **Marie-Pierre seemed to be asking:** When I double-checked this quote with Marie-Pierre and asked for her permission to use it here (which included sending her a scanned copy of the original note) she reported that she meant it to read "the asshole strikes again." At least half a dozen people whom I showed her note to also read it as "the asshole shits again" and Marie-Pierre agreed that in her handwriting "strikes" looked much like "shits."

4 **The prevalence of asshole bosses:** The Workplace Bullying Institute's U.S. Workplace Bullying Survey. http://www. workplacebullying.org/research/WBI-Zogby2007Survey.html (accessed August 10, 2009). The University of Florida research is summarized by Jeanna Bryner, "Abused Workers Fight Back by Slacking Off," *Live Science*, October 8, 2007. http://www.livescience.com/health/071008-abusive-bosses. html (accessed August 11, 2009).

7 **My conclusions and advice:** Unless otherwise noted, all examples and evidence in this book are factual. They are based on published sources and academic studies, stories that others have told me, and my own experiences. I have gone to great lengths to check multiple sources when using published stories and studies, to double-check my own recollections with others who were present, and to have most stories that others told me checked and corrected by the person who originally told me the story. Yet despite such efforts, the recollections reported here (both mine and others) are no doubt imperfect given the flaws and biases that haunt every human being's brain. Moreover, on fewer than five occasions, I have changed people's names or other identifying information (e.g., gender) to protect the innocent and the guilty, although in all cases the facts in these examples are otherwise unaltered.

8 **Eleanor Roosevelt:** Quoted on the website The Quotations Page. http://www.quotationspage.com/quote/38694.html (accessed August 31, 2009). Note that this saying is attributed to Eleanor Roosevelt on dozens of websites and it appears to come from a poem that is attributed to her, however I am unable to find the original source.

8 **The cautionary tales:** Amanda Royal, "Pillsbury Confirms Layoff Leak," *Recorder*, February 20, 2009. http://www.law. com/jsp/article.jsp?id=1202428436200 (accessed August 11, 2009).

Chapter 1

13 **21 million bosses:** U.S. Labor Statistics Bureau, *2008–2009 Occupational Outlook Handbook* (Washington, DC, January 2008). This handbook describes approximately 800 occupations and estimates the number of employees in each. Stanford doctoral student Isaac Waisberg classified 47 of these occupations as bosses, which we defined as wielding authority over at least one subordinate. Waisberg estimated that 20,891,000 of the 134,354,280 employees in these occupations fit this definition. Other estimates based on these data run as high as 37.7 million bosses. See "Boss Day is Moving Up the Ladder Among Cardgivers," *Kansas City Business Journal*, October 8, 2004. http://kansascity.bizjournals.com/kansascity/stories/2004/10/04/daily35.html (accessed August 11, 2009). Waisberg estimated that over 90 percent of U.S. workers have bosses, as there were about 10,200,000 self-employed people in the U.S.—people who often don't have bosses.

13 **Early in my career:** I learned about these two bosses when I worked with SPaM in the 1990s. This text was reviewed and confirmed by Corey Billington via e-mail on December 16, 2008.

15 **A Swedish study:** Anna Nyberg and others, "Managerial Leadership and Ischaemic Heart Disease Among Employees: The Swedish WOLF Study," *Occupational and Environmental Medicine* 66 (2009): 51–55. Anna Nyberg quote from Frances Schwartzkopff, "Bad Bosses Raise Heart Attack Risk for Men, Researchers Find," Bloomberg.com. http://www.bloomberg.com/apps/news?pid=20601080&sid=apuGRus9J2q4&refer=asia (accessed August 11, 2009).

15 **Researcher Robert Hogan:** Robert Hogan, *Personality and the Fate of Organizations* (Mahwah, NJ: Lawrence Erlbaum Associates), 106.

16 **Bosses make the biggest difference:** Robert T. Keller, "Transformational Leadership, Initiating Structure, and

Substitutes for Leadership: A Longitudinal Study of Research and Development Project Team Performance," *Journal of Applied Psychology* 91, no. 1 (2006): 202–210.

16 **Sports teams:** Lawrence M. Kahn, "Managerial Quality, Team Success, and Individual Player Performance in Major League Baseball," *Industrial and Labor Relations Review* 46 (1993): 531–547; Jeffrey Pfeffer and Alison Davis-Blake, "Administrative Succession and Organizational Performance: How Administrator Experience Mediates the Succession Effect," *Academy of Management Journal* 29, no. 1 (1986): 72–83; and Amanda Goodall, Lawrence M. Kahn, and Andrew J. Oswald, "Why Do Leaders Matter? The Role of Expert Knowledge," IZA Discussion Paper No. 3583, Social Science Research Network, http://papers.ssrn.com/sol3/papers.cfm?abstract_id=1158980.

17 **Bosses mattered massively:** See Marcus Buckingham and Curt Coffman, *First, Break All the Rules* (New York: Simon & Schuster, 1999). The quote "managers trump companies" is on page 34. Also see Hogan, *Personality and the fate of organizations*, 38. Material about the 2007 study and the remaining quotes are from "Many Employees Would Fire Their Boss," *Gallup Management Journal* press release, October 11, 2007, http://gmj.gallup.com/content/28867/Many-Employees-Would-Fire-Their-Boss.aspx (accessed August 11, 2009).

18 **The ways that senior leaders treat direct reports:** Michael D. Ensley, Keith M. Hmieleski, and Craig L. Pearce, "The Importance of Vertical and Shared Leadership Within New Venture Top Management Teams: Implications for the Performance of Startups," *The Leadership Quarterly* 17 (2006): 217–231; Sydney Finkelstein and Donald C. Hambrick, *Strategic Leadership: Top Executives and Their Effects on Organizations* (Minneapolis/St. Paul: West, 1996); Mason A. Carpenter and William Gerard Sanders, "Top Management Team Compensation: The Missing Link

Between CEO Pay and Firm Performance?" *Strategic Management Journal* 4 (2002): 367–375; Kathleen M. Eisenhardt, Jean L. Kahwajy, and L. J. Bourgeois III, "How Management Teams Can Have a Good Fight," *Harvard Business Review* (July–August 1997): 77–85; and Doris Kearns Goodwin, *Team of Rivals* (New York: Simon & Schuster, 2005).

21 **Lasorda once said:** Tommy Lasorda and David Fisher, *The Artful Dodger* (New York: Avon, 1986), 244. Also see Daniel R. Ames and Francis J. Flynn, "What Breaks a Leader: The Curvilinear Relation Between Assertiveness and Leadership," *Journal of Personality and Social Psychology* 92 (2007): 308.

22 **Experiments at Stanford:** Jeffrey Pfeffer and others, "Faith in Supervision and The Self-Enhancement Bias: Two Psychological Reasons Why Managers Don't Empower Workers," *Basic and Applied Social Psychology* 20 (1998): 313–321.

23 **As he put it:** Robert I. Sutton, *Weird Ideas That Work* (New York: Free Press, 2001), 127.

23 **Frank Hauser offered:** Frank Hauser and Russell Reich, *Notes on Directing* (New York: Walker), 9.

24 **Researchers use the word *grit*:** Angela L. Duckworth and others, "Grit: Perseverance and Passion for Long-Term Goals," *Journal of Personality and Social Psychology* 92 (2007): 1087–1101. The Albert Einstein quotes can be found at http://www.brainyquote.com/quotes/quotes/a/alberteins106192.html (accessed August 14, 2009), but may be apocryphal as I am unable to find the original source.

24 **Glenn Osaka has grit:** This story first appeared (in a longer form and with different language) in Jeffrey Pfeffer and Robert I. Sutton, *Hard Facts, Dangerous Half-Truths, and Total Nonsense* (Boston: Harvard Business School Press), 182.

25 **Pixar's Brad Bird:** Brad Bird, interview by Hayagreeva Rao, Allen P. Webb, and the author, Emeryville, California, February 14, 2008. Quotes are from the original transcript.

Excerpts appeared in Hayagreeva Rao, Robert Sutton, and Allen P. Webb, "Innovation Lessons from Pixar: An Interview with Oscar-Winning Director Brad Bird," *McKinsey Quarterly* (April 2008), http://www.mckinseyquarterly.com/innovation_lessons_from_pixar_an_interview_with_oscar-winning_director_brad_bird_2127 (accessed August 11, 2009).

26 **This nagging conviction:** "Scenes from a Mall," *This American Life*, episode 371, Chicago Public Radio, December 26, 2008, http://www.thisamericanlife.org/Radio_Episode.aspx?sched=1276 (accessed August 11, 2009).

27 **Small Wins:** Karl E. Weick, "Small Wins: Redefining the Scale of Social Problems," *American Psychologist* 39 (1984): 40–49.

28 **Consider Andy Papathanassiou:** Andy Papathanassiou, telephone interview by author, December 10, 2008.

31 **Anthropologists who study chimpanzees:** Lionel Tiger, "Dominance in Human Societies," *Annual Review of Ecology and Systematics* 1 (1970): 298.

31 **Psychologist Susan Fiske observes:** Susan T. Fiske, "Controlling Other People: The Impact of Power on Stereotyping," *American Psychologist* 48 (1993): 624.

31 **Kelley Eskridge:** Kelley Eskridge, "They Watch Everything You Do," Humans at Work, November 7, 2008, http://www.humansatwork.com/they-watch-everything-you-do/ (accessed August 13, 2009).

32 **Linda Hudson...learned:** Adam Bryant, "Fitting In, and Rising to the Top," Corner Office, *New York Times*, September 19, 2009, http://www.nytimes.com/2009/09/20/business/20corner.html (accessed October 13, 2009).

33 **power poisoning:** Dacher Keltner, Deborah H. Gruenfeld, and Cameron Anderson, "Power, Approach, and Inhibition," *Psychological Review* 110 (2003): 265–284.

34 **The advice that David Packard:** "Dave Packard's 11 Simple Rules," HP Retiree, http://www.hp.com/retiree/history/founders/packard/11rules.html (accessed August 13, 2009).

34 **Donovan Campbell led:** Donovan Campbell, *Joker One* (New York: Random House, 2009), 221.

38 **I am singing a tune:** Mark Van Vugt, Robert Hogan, and Robert B. Kaiser, "Leadership, Followership, and Evolution: Some Lessons from the Past," *American Psychologist* 63 (2008): 190.

39 **"self-enhancement bias":** Jeffrey Pfeffer and Christina T. Fong, "Building Organization Theory from First Principles: The Self-Enhancement Motive and Understanding Power and Influence," *Organization Science* 16 (2005): 372; O. Svensen, "Are We All Risky and More Skillful Than Our Fellow Drivers?" *Acta Psychologia* 47 (1981): 143–148; and Jim Collins, *Good to Great* (New York: HarperBusiness, 2001).

39 **the College Board's survey:** The research in this paragraph and the related findings about inflated self-assessments are reviewed in David Dunning, Chip Heath, and Jerry M. Suls, "Flawed Self-Assessment: Implications for Health, Education, and the Workplace," *Psychological Science* 5 (2004): 69–106; and in David Dunning, *Self-Insight* (New York: Psychology Press, 2005).

40 **Performance:** J. Richard Hackman, *Leading Teams* (Boston: Harvard Business School Press, 2002); and Robert Townsend, *Up the Organization* (1970; repr., San Francisco: Jossey-Bass, 2007).

41 **Humanity:** Randy Hodson, *Dignity at Work* (Cambridge: Cambridge University Press, 2001).

41 **Dr. Michael Giuliano asserted:** Michael Giuliano, "Diagnostic Error in the NICU: Not in My NICU?" (presented at the NICU Quality Improvement Collaborative, Vermont Oxford Network, San Francisco, September 10, 2008).

42 **This notion is conveyed simply:** David Kelley did this drawing and we discussed this balancing act on June 17, 2009, at IDEO in Palo Alto, California.

43 ***Zen in the Art of Archery* shows:** Eugen Herrigal, *Zen in the Art of Archery* (New York: Vintage, 1971).

Chapter 2

47 **Research by James Meindl:** James R. Meindl, Sanford B. Ehrlich, and Janet M. Dukerich, "The Romance of Leadership," *Administrative Science Quarterly* 30 (1985): 78–102.

49 **The truth is that bosses:** See Pfeffer and Sutton, *Hard Facts*, chapter 8; and Roberto Weber and others, "The Illusion of Leadership: Misattribution of Cause in Coordination Games," *Organization Science* 12 (2001): 582–598.

50 **As Max DePree:** Max DePree, *Leadership Is an Art* (New York: Broadway Business, 2001), 11.

50 **Andy Grove was tremendously successful:** Andy Grove, interview by Clayton Christensen, Harvard Business School Conference, Cupertino, California, October 3, 2002. I attended this session, and the organizers provided me a transcript.

51 **"belief follows behavior":** Philip G. Zimbardo and Michael R. Leippe, *The Psychology of Attitude Change and Social Influence* (New York: McGraw-Hill, 1991); and Elaine Hatfield, John T. Cacioppo, and Richard L. Rapson, *Emotional Contagion* (Cambridge: Cambridge University Press, 1993).

51 **Washington made many mistakes:** David McCullough, *1776* (New York: Simon & Schuster, 2006), 42–43.

52 **Goldman Sachs CEO Lloyd Blankfein:** Adam Bryant, "Lessons Learned at Goldman," Corner Office, *New York Times*, September 13, 2009, http://www.nytimes.com/2009/09/13/business/13corner.html (accessed October 6, 2009).

53 **Consider Bill Campbell's experience:** From conversations between Randy Komisar and me, notably between February 17, 2009, and February 24, 2009. Also see Jennifer Reingold, "The Secret Coach," *Fortune*, July 21, 2008, http://money.cnn.com/2008/07/21/technology/reingold_coach.fortune/index.htm (accessed August 14, 2009).

54 **Teeter-Totter Syndrome:** Laurence J. Peter and Raymond
Hull, *The Peter Principle* (1969; repr., New York: Collins
Business, 2009), 107.

55 **I love the advice:** Hauser and Reich, *Notes on Directing,* 45.

58 **"overclaiming":** Max H. Bazerman and Don Moore,
Judgment in Managerial Decision Making, 7th ed.
(Hoboken, NJ: Wiley, 2009).

58 ***BusinessWeek* approached IDEO:** I heard this story from
Kelley as it unfolded in 2000 and he confirmed the facts on
June 17, 2009. Also see Bruce Nussbaum, "Welcome to 2010,"
BusinessWeek, March 6, 2000, http://www.businessweek.
com/2000/00_10/designtoc.htm (accessed August 14, 2009).

60 **In late August 2008:** Terence Flynn, "Authentic Crisis
Leadership and Reputation Management: Maple Leaf Foods
and 2008 Listeriosis Crisis" (unpublished manuscript,
DeGroote School of Business, McMaster University, 2009),
http://www.degroote.mcmaster.ca/news/documents/
DeGrooteLegerAuthenticCrisisLeadershipPaperfinal.pdf
(accessed August 14, 2009). Also see Sylvain Charlebois,
"Maple Leaf Foods Showed That Leadership Can Prevail in
Trying Times," FP Executive, *Financial Post*, January 9, 2009,
http://www.financialpost.com/executive/story.
html?id=1159895 (accessed August 14, 2009); and Steve
Arnold, "Coming Clean Helped Maple Leaf," *Hamilton
Spectator*, January 30, 2009, http://www.thespec.com/
article/504360 (accessed August 14, 2009).

61 **Another misguided trick:** William Safire, *Safire's Political
Dictionary* (New York: Oxford, 2008), 431.

61 **Chairman of the Board J. R. Crespo:** "Mistakes Were
Made," *New Haven Independent*, March 12, 2007, http://
www.newhavenindependent.org/archives/2007/03/read_it_
yoursel.php (accessed August 14, 2009).

62 **If you as a boss want to enhance the illusion:** Fiona Lee
and Robert J. Robinson, "An Attributional Analysis of Social
Accounts: Implications of Playing the Blame Game," *Journal*

of Applied Social Psychology 30 (2000): 1853–1879; Fiona Lee and Larissa Z. Tiedens, "Who's Being Served? Self-Serving Attributions and Their Implications for Power," *Organizational Behavior and Human Decision Processes* 84 (2001): 254–287; Gerald R. Salancik and James R. Meindl, "Corporate Attributions as Strategic Illusions of Management Control," *Administrative Science Quarterly* 29 (1984): 238–254; and Fiona Lee, Christopher Peterson, and Larissa Z. Tiedens, "Mea Culpa: Predicting Stock Prices from Organizational Attributions," *Personality and Social Psychology Bulletin* 30 (2004): 1–14.

64　**Barbara Kellerman shows:** Barbara Kellerman, "When Should a Leader Apologize—and When Not?" *Harvard Business Review* 84, no. 4 (2006): 71.

66　**Joe Torre managed:** Joe Torre and Tom Verducci, *The Yankee Years* (New York: Doubleday, 2009); and "If Dodgers Falter, Torre Says Blame Him," quote from the *San Bernardino Sun* on Baseball Think Factory, June 2, 2009, http://www.baseballthinkfactory.org/files/newsstand/ discussion/if_dodgers_falter_torre_says_blame_him/ (accessed August 14, 2009).

68　**Talk more than others:** Bernard M. Bass, *Bass & Stogdill's Handbook of Leadership*, 3rd ed. (New York: Free Press, 1990), 90–94.

68　**Interrupt people:** This is a delicate balance as subordinates dislike bosses who interrupt them constantly, but interrupting others is a hallmark of powerful people. See Lynn Smith-Lovin and Charles Brody, "Interruptions in Group Discussions: The Effects of Gender and Group Composition," *American Sociological Review* 54 (1989): 424–435.

68　**Cross your arms:** Ron Friedman and Andrew J. Elliot, "The Effect of Arm Crossing on Persistence and Performance," *European Journal of Social Psychology* 38 (2008): 449–461.

69　**Use positive self-talk:** Chris P. Neck and Charles C. Manz, "Thought Self-Leadership: The Influence of Self-Talk and

Mental Imagery on Performance, *Journal of Organizational Behavior* 13 (1992): 681–699.

69 **Try a little flash of anger:** Larissa Z. Tiedens, "Anger and Advancement Versus Sadness and Subjugation: The Effect of Negative Emotion Expressions on Social Status Conferral," *Journal of Personality and Social Psychology* 80 (2001): 86–94; and Marwan Sinaceur and Larissa Z. Tiedens, "Get Mad and Get More Than Even: When and Why Anger Expression Is Effective in Negotiations," *Journal of Experimental Social Psychology* 42 (2006): 314–322.

69 **stand up:** Barry Schwartz, Abraham Tesser, and Evan Powell, "Dominance Cues in Nonverbal Behavior," *Social Psychology Quarterly* 45 (1982): 114–120.

69 **Tell people about your pet peeves:** Ben Dattner, "A User's Manual: To You," Business at Work: Toxic Bosses, *BusinessWeek*, August 13, 2008, http://www.businessweek.com/business_at_work/bad_bosses/archives/2008/08/a_managerial_us.html (accessed August 14, 2009).

Chapter 3

72 **Coach John Wooden's advice:** John Wooden with Steve Jamison, *Wooden* (New York: McGraw Hill, 1997), 117.

72 **Wisdom:** John A. Meacham, "The Loss of Wisdom," in *Wisdom*, ed. Robert J. Sternberg, 181–211 (New York: Cambridge University Press, 1990); and Karl E. Weick, "The Collapse of Sensemaking in Organizations: The Mann Gulch Disaster," *Administrative Science Quarterly* 38 (1993): 628–652. Also, the notion that wise people have "strong opinions, weakly held" was developed by Paul Saffo when he worked for the Institute for the Future in Palo Alto, California. Jeff Pfeffer and I also presented earlier versions of these ideas in Pfeffer and Sutton, *Hard Facts,* chapter 4.

74 **Many of the skilled bosses:** Hauser and Reich, *Notes on Directing,* 45; McCullough, *1776,* 42–43; and Andy Grove interview.

74 **Psychological safety:** Amy C. Edmondson, "Learning from Mistakes Is Easier Said Than Done: Group and Organizational Influences on the Detection and Correction of Human Error," *Journal of Applied Behavioral Science* 32 (1996): 5–28; and Anita L. Tucker and Amy C. Edmondson, "Why Hospitals Don't Learn from Failures: Organizational and Psychological Dynamics That Inhibit System Change," *California Management Review* 45 (2003): 55–72.

75 **Giuliano urges doctors:** Giuliano, "Diagnostic Error in the NICU."

76 **A study in flight simulators:** H. Clayton Foushee, "Dyads and Triads at 35,000 Feet: Factors Affecting Group Process and Aircrew Performance," *American Psychologist* 39 (1984): 885–893.

77 **Jeff Pfeffer and I argue:** Pfeffer and Sutton, *Hard Facts,* 232–234.

78 **IDEO's Diego Rodriguez:** Diego Rodriguez, "Where Is Your Place for Failing?" Metacool, November 21, 2007, http://metacool.typepad.com/metacool/2007/11/heard-at-work.html (accessed August 19, 2009).

79 **The writers of *The Onion*:** Wells Tower, "Onion Nation," *Washington Post*, November 16, 2008, http://www.washingtonpost.com/wp-dyn/content/article/2008/11/07/AR2008110701942.html (accessed August 19, 2009); and "Tough Room," *This American Life*, episode 348, Chicago Public Radio, February 8, 2008, http://www.thisamericanlife.org/Radio_Episode.aspx?episode=348 (accessed August 19, 2009).

80 **The fallacy of centrality:** Ron Westrum, "Social Intelligence About Hidden Events," *Knowledge* 3 (1982): 381–400. Karl E. Weick and Kathleen M. Sutcliff, *Managing the Unexpected* (San Francisco: Jossey-Bass, 2007), 158.

80 **Most bosses are too busy:** Sidney Rosen and Abraham Tesser, "On Reluctance to Communicate Undesirable Information: The MUM Effect," *Sociometry* 33 (1970):

253–263; and Michael Lewis, "The Man Who Crashed the World," *Vanity Fair*, August 2009, http://www.vanityfair.com/politics/features/2009/08/aig200908?currentPage=3 (accessed August 19, 2009).

82 **Veteran project manager:** Paul F. Snare, *Tales from the Project Trade* (Victoria, BC: Trafford, 2002), 13, 15.

82 **People are especially prone:** Karl E. Weick and Kathleen M. Sutcliffe, *Managing the Unexpected* (San Francisco: Jossey-Bass, 2007), 63. The information from Warner-Simi is from e-mail exchanges I had with her March 5–6, 2009.

83 **Wise bosses like a good fight:** Eisenhardt, Kahwajy, and Bourgeois, "How Management Teams Can Have a Good Fight"; and Karen A. Jehn, "A Multi-Method Examination of the Benefits and Detriments of Intragroup Conflicts," *Administrative Science Quarterly* 40 (1995): 256–282. The Weick quote is from Robert I. Sutton, *The No Asshole Rule* (New York: Business Plus, 2007), 81.

85 **Brad Bird:** Brad Bird interview.

88 **"Fight for what you believe, but gracefully accept defeat":** Lamont Adams, "Download the Builder.com Ten Commandments of Egoless Programming," TechRepublic, June 6, 2002, http://articles.techrepublic.com.com/5100-10878_11-1045782.html (accessed August 20, 2009).

89 **The first trap:** "The Surplus," *The Office,* episode 75, NBC, December 4, 2008, directed by Paul Feig and written by Gene Stupnitsky and Lee Eisenberg.

89 **The second trap:** Ingrid Nembhard and others, "Learn How to Improve Collaboration and Performance" (Harvard Business School Working Paper no. 08-002, 2007). A summary of this paper is available at http://www.evidence-basedmanagement.com/guests/nembhard_tucker_bohmer_horbar_carpenter_jan08.html (accessed August 20, 2009).

90 **"let workers work":** Jeffrey Pfeffer, *What Were They Thinking?* (Boston: Harvard Business School Press, 2007), 56.

92 **Margie Mauldin, an executive coach:** Bob Sutton, "The

Tape Method," Work Matters, August 14, 2008, http://
bobsutton.typepad.com/my_weblog/2008/08/the-tape-
method.html (accessed August 20, 2009).

93 **When Xerox promoted Anne Mulcahy:** William George
and Andrew N. McLean, "Anne Mulcahy: Leading Xerox
Through the Perfect Storm (A)," Case 9-405-050 (Boston:
Harvard Business School, 2005), 8.

96 **Robert Townsend:** Townsend, *Up the Organization*, 129.

96 **Max DePree:** DePree, *Leadership Is an Art*, 11.

96 **"the attitude of gratitude":** Kimberly Wiefling, *Scrappy
Project Management* (Cupertino, CA: Happy About,
2007), 113.

Chapter 4

99 **"They tout the 'no-a**hole rule' ":** "100 Best Companies to
Work for 2008," *Fortune*, http://money.cnn.com/magazines/
fortune/bestcompanies/2008/snapshots/39.html (accessed
August 20, 2009); and Paul Purcell, telephone interview by
author, March 20, 2008; "100 Best Companies to Work for
2010," *Fortune*, http://money.cnn.com/magazines/fortune/
bestcompanies/2010/snapshots/11.html (accessed February
15, 2010). Also see Bob Sutton, "Details on the No Asshole
Rule at Robert W. Baird: #39 on *Fortune*'s '100 Best
Companies to Work for' List," Work Matters, http://
bobsutton.typepad.com/my_weblog/2008/03/details-on-the.
html (accessed August 20, 2009).

101 **"We don't accomplish anything in this world alone":**
Ann Carey McFeatters, *Sandra Day O'Connor: Justice in the
Balance* (Albuquerque, NM: University of New Mexico
Press, 2006), 1.

101 **"Hell is just other people":** Jean-Paul Sartre, *No Exit: A
Play in One Act* (New York: Samuel French, 1958), 52.

102 **And the most talented people:** Dean Keith Simonton,
Greatness (New York: Guilford, 1994); and Frank L. Schmidt
and John E. Hunter, "The Validity and Utility of Selection

Methods in Personnel Psychology: Practical and Theoretical Implications of 85 Years of Research Findings," *Psychological Bulletin* 124 (1998): 262–274.

102 **Men's Wearhouse:** Charles A. O'Reilly III and Jeffrey Pfeffer, *Hidden Value* (Boston: Harvard Business School Press, 2000), 90.

103 **Morten Hansen shows:** Morten T. Hansen, *Collaboration* (Boston: Harvard Business School Press, 2009).

105 **what Steve Kerr called:** Steven Kerr, "On the Folly of Rewarding A, While Hoping for B," *Academy of Management Executive* 9 (1995): 7–14.

105 **Merrill Lynch:** Paul Stiles, *Riding the Bull* (New York: Random House, 1998); and Dan Heath and Chip Heath, "Why Incentives are Effective, Irresistible, and Almost Certain to Backfire," *Fast Company*, January 15, 2009, http://www.fastcompany.com/magazine/132/made-to-stick-curse-of-incentives.html (accessed August 21, 2009).

106 **Harry S. Truman:** Richard Alan Krieger, *Civilization's Quotations* (New York: Algora, 2002), 218.

107 **A. G. Lafley:** Patricia Sellers, "P&G: Teaching an Old Dog New Tricks: CEO A. G. Lafley Has Kicked Up the Good Ideas at the Stodgy Midwestern Giant—and the Company's Growth Too. Here's an Inside Look at How He's Doing It," *Fortune*, May 31, 2004, http://money.cnn.com/magazines/fortune/fortune_archive/2004/05/31/370714/index.htm (accessed August 21, 2009).

107 **General Electric executives:** For an explanation and defense of the GE system see Jack Welch and John A. Byrne, *Jack* (New York: Business Plus, 2001). This research is reviewed in Pfeffer and Sutton, *Hard Facts*, chapters 4 and 5.

108 **Rob Cross studies social networks:** Robert L. Cross and Andrew Parker, *The Hidden Power of Social Networks* (Boston: Harvard Business School Press, 2004), 49.

110 **Gordon MacKenzie:** Gordon MacKenzie, *Orbiting the Giant Hairball* (New York: Penguin, 1996). The quote is

from Anna Muoio's interview with MacKenzie, "How Is Your Company Like a Giant Hairball?" *Fast Company,* December 31, 1997, http://www.fastcompany.com/magazine/12/hairball.html (accessed February 24, 2010).

111 **accentuating the positive isn't enough:** Will Felps, Terence R. Mitchell, and Eliza Byington, "How, When, and Why Bad Apples Spoil the Barrel: Negative Group Members and Dysfunctional Groups," *Research in Organizational Behavior* 27 (2006): 175–222. Also see "Ruining It for the Rest of Us," *This American Life,* episode 370, December 19, 2008, http://www.thisamericanlife.org/radio_episode.aspx?sched=1275 (accessed August 23, 2009).

112 **"bad is stronger than good":** Roy F. Baumeister and others, "Bad Is Stronger Than Good," *Review of General Psychology* 5 (2001): 323–370.

113 **Exhibit #1 is performance evaluations:** Bob Sutton, "Performance Evaluations: Do They Do More Harm Than Good?" Work Matters, February 15, 2008, http://bobsutton.typepad.com/my_weblog/2008/02/perfromnce-eval.html (accessed August 23, 2009); and Samuel A. Culbert, "Get rid of the performance review!" *Wall Street Journal,* October 20, 2008, F4.

115 **drill instructors:** Dov Eden and Abraham B. Shani, "Pygmalion Goes to Boot Camp: Expectancy, Leadership and Trainee Performance," *Journal of Applied Psychology* 67 (1982): 197.

116 **"Do you need a group of both winners and losers?":** Dov Eden, "Pygmalion Without Interpersonal Contrast Effects: Whole Groups Gain from Raising Manager Expectations," *Journal of Applied Psychology* 75 (1990): 394–398. The quote about Southwest Airlines is from "Company Culture: Out of the Ordinary," *The Excellence Files,* DVD (Lakewood, WA: The Richardson Co. Training Media, 1997).

117 **Psychologists call this confirmation bias:** "Confirmation

Bias," The Skeptic's Dictionary, http://www.skepdic.com/ confirmbias.html (accessed September 1, 2009).

117   **confirmation bias can blind you:** Barry M. Staw and Ha Hoang, "Sunk Costs in the NBA: Why Draft Order Affects Playing Time and Survival in Professional Basketball," *Administrative Science Quarterly* 40 (1995): 474–494.

118   **U.S. women's national soccer team:** Jere Longman, *The Girls of Summer* (New York: HarperCollins, 2000).

119   **virtues of "hard teams":** Kathleen M. Eisenhardt and Claudia Bird Schoonhoven, "Organizational Growth: Linking Founding Team, Strategy, Environment, and Growth Among U.S. Semiconductor Ventures, 1978–1988," *Administrative Science Quarterly* 35 (1990): 504–529; and J. Richard Hackman, *Leading Teams* (Boston: Harvard Business School Press, 2002), 54–59.

121   **A manager in a semiconductor company:** Sutton, *Weird Ideas That Work*, 39–40.

123   **Sgt. John Ludden:** Wally Bock told me this story, and corrected and revised facts, via e-mail exchanges on January 11–12, 2009.

Chapter 5

127   **The "smart-talk trap":** Jeffrey Pfeffer and Robert I. Sutton, "The Smart-Talk Trap," *Harvard Business Review* 77, no. 3 (1999): 134–142.

128   **I asked Pixar's:** Brad Bird interview.

129   **Respect:** "Enron Code of Ethics," July 2000, available at The Smoking Gun, http://www.thesmokinggun.com/enron/ enronethics1.html (accessed August 23, 2009).

129   **Jeff Pfeffer and I wrote:** Jeffrey Pfeffer and Robert I. Sutton, *The Knowing-Doing Gap* (Boston: Harvard Business School Press, 2000).

130   **Don't let your people:** Bass, *Bass & Stogdill's Handbook of Leadership*, 3rd ed., 90–94.

131   **Matthew May describes a dirty trick:** May's story is from

Bob Sutton, "More on the Broken Culture in the Auto Industry: How Dysfunctional Power Dynamics Cause Bad Decisions," Work Matters, November 24, 2008, http://bobsutton.typepad.com/my_weblog/2008/11/more-on-the-broken-culture-in-the-auto-industry-how-dysfunctional-power-dynamics-cause-bad-decisions.html (accessed August 23, 2009).

133 **After Kroc bought the franchise rights:** John F. Love, *McDonald's: Behind the Arches* (New York: Bantam, 1995), 71.

133 **You don't have to be a founder or CEO:** Rudy Crespo gave me this tour on July 17, 2009. The facts given here were confirmed via e-mails with Mr. Crespo on March 14 and March 17, 2009.

134 **Every boss can't have deep knowledge:** Gerald M. Weinberg, *The Psychology of Computer Programming* (New York: Dorset, 1998), 80.

135 **One reason that General Motors:** This description of the program is based on conversations with three anonymous former GM employees who participated in the program, assorted past conversations with people who worked at GM and partook in it, and this media report: Hoffman, B.G. (2209) "Lease Perks Anger Workers," *The Detroit News*, 10/30/08, page 1. Also see my blog post at Work Matters, "The Auto Industry Bailout: Thoughts About Why GM Executives Are Clueless and Their Destructive 'No We Can't' Mindset," November 24, 2008, http://bobsutton.typepad.com/my_weblog/2008/11/the-auto-industry-bailout-thoughts-about-why-gm-executives-are-clueless-and-their-no-we-cant-mindset.html (accessed August 23, 2009).

137 **To illustrate, SYPartners:** SYP's Lisa Maulhardt told this story during a talk to executives at Stanford University on November 18, 2008. I followed up with Lisa to learn more and do fact-checking in an e-mail exchange between July 6 and July 20, 2009.

139 **"Brace, brace, heads down, stay down":** Mark Mooney and Jonann Brady, "'Sully' Sullenberg Meets Grateful

Passengers," ABC News, February 9, 2009, http://abcnews.go.com/US/story?id=6834954&page=1 (accessed August 23, 2009).

139   **The power of concreteness:** Lee Ross and Richard E. Nisbett, *The Person and the Situation* (New York: McGraw-Hill, 1991), 90–91.

140   **Checklists create especially strong connective tissue:** Atul Gawande, "The Checklist," *The New Yorker*, December 10, 2007, http://www.newyorker.com/reporting/2007/12/10/071210 fa_fact_gawande (accessed August 23, 2009).

141   **unintelligible language:** Donald H. Naftulin, John E. Ware Jr., and Frank A. Donnelly, "The Doctor Fox Lecture: A Paradigm of Educational Seduction," *Journal of Medical Education* 48 (1973): 630–635.

141   **"the curse of knowledge":** Pamela J. Hinds, "The Curse of Expertise: The Effects of Expertise and Debiasing Methods on Predictions of Novice Performance," *Journal of Experimental Psychology: Applied* 5 (1999): 205–221.

142   **"Keep It Simple, Stupid":** Richard Williams, *The Animator's Survival Kit* (London: Faber & Faber, 2002).

143   **Chip and Dan Heath teach us:** Chip Heath and Dan Heath, *Made to Stick* (New York: Random House, 2007).

143   **Conrad Hilton:** I have not seen this *Tonight Show* episode and cannot find a completely reliable source to confirm it. Available versions of the story can be found in Werner Herzog, *Herzog on Herzog*, ed. Paul Cronin (London: Faber and Faber, 2002), 1; and Tim Pawlenty, "Shaping K-12 Education," in *The Challenges of School Reform*, ed. Lewis C. Solmon, Kimberly Firetag Agam, and Citadelle Priagula (Charlotte, NC: IAP—Information Age Publishing, 2006), 221.

143   **Otis Redding Problem:** Pfeffer and Sutton, *The Knowing-Doing Gap*, 140.

144   **COO Joe Mello:** Bob Sutton, "No Brag, Just Facts at DaVita," Work Matters, September 16, 2006, http://bobsutton.

typepad.com/my_weblog/2006/09/no_brag_just_fa.html (accessed August 23, 2009).

145   **When Jobs took over Apple:** Pfeffer and Sutton, "The Smart-Talk Trap," 140–141.

146   **Timbuk2:** For part of the story, see Jessie Scanlon, "How to Make Meetings Matter," *BusinessWeek* Online, April 28, 2008, http://www.businessweek.com/innovate/content/apr2008/id20080428_601886.htm (accessed August 23, 2009).

148   **Walt Disney:** Retrieved from "Walt Disney Quotes," Finest Quotes, http://www.finestquotes.com/author_quotes-author-Walt%20Disney-page-0.htm (accessed November 23, 2009).

148   **Keysha Cooper:** Gretchen Morgenson, "Was There a Loan It Didn't Like?" *New York Times*, November 1, 2008, http://www.nytimes.com/2008/11/02/business/02gret.html (accessed August 23, 2009).

150   **Maytag bought a struggling San Francisco brewery:** Hayagreeva Rao, *Market Rebels* (Princeton: Princeton University Press, 2009, 55.

Chapter 6

154   **management "buffers":** James D. Thompson, *Organizations in Action* (New York: McGraw-Hill, 1967).

154   **Robert Townsend could have been:** Townsend, *Up the Organization*, 163, 169.

155   **Captain Nick Gottuso:** Nick Gottuso, interview by author, Hillsborough, California, January 15, 2009; Gottuso checked and corrected facts in an e-mail exchange with the author on November 19, 2009. For a description of the hostage situation and murder see Tyche Hendricks and Matthew B. Stannard, "Mother, Intruder Killed in Peninsula Home," *San Francisco Chronicle*, November 26, 2008, http://www.sfgate.com/cgi-bin/article.cgi?f=/c/a/2008/11/25/MN0U14C53M.DTL (accessed November 20, 2009).

157   **Merina tribe:** Maurice Bloch, "Decision-Making in Councils Among the Merina of Madagascar," in *Cambridge Papers in Social Anthropology,* vol. 6, *Councils in Action,* ed. Audrey Richards and Adam Kuper (New York: Cambridge University Press, 1971), 29–62.

159   **Will Wright:** Adam Bryant, "On His Team, Would You Be a Solvent, or the Glue?" *New York Times,* June 12, 2009, http://www.nytimes.com/2009/06/14/business/14corner.html?pagewanted=1&_r=1 (accessed August 25, 2009).

161   **Research on stand-up meetings:** Allen C. Bluedorn, Daniel B. Turban, and Mary Sue Love, "The Effects of Stand-Up and Sit-Down Meeting Formats on Meeting Outcomes," *Journal of Applied Psychology* 84 (1999): 277–285.

161   **Robert Townsend advised:** Townsend, *Up the Organization,* 130.

161   **David Darragh:** Mr. Darragh told me about his stand-up meetings during a conversation in Northern California on September 24, 2008. I followed up with him via e-mail to get more details and clarify facts on December 6 and December 11, 2008.

163   **"Someone once defined a manager":** Henry Mintzberg, "The Manager's Job: Folklore and Fact," *Harvard Business Review* 68, no. 2 (1990): 165. This article was originally published in 1975.

163   **A study of manufacturing foremen:** R.H. Guest, "Of Time and Foreman," *Personnel* 32 (1956): 478–486.

164   **Research by Gloria Mark:** Gloria Mark, Victor M. Gonzalez, and Justin Harris, "No Task Left Behind? Examining the Nature of Fragmented Work" (paper, CHI 2005, Portland, OR, April 2–7, 2005), 113–120; and Gloria Mark, Daniela Gudith, and Ulrich Klocke, "The Cost of Interrupted Work: More Speed and Stress," in *Proceedings of the Twenty-Sixth Annual SIGCHI Conference on Human Factors in Computing Systems* (New York: ACM, 2008), 107–110.

165 **In 2007, Bonny and her management team:** From conversations and e-mails with Ms. Warner-Simi in late 2008 and 2009, especially on December 12, 2008.

167 **3M CEO William McKnight:** W. Coyne, "3M: Vision Is the Engine That Drives Our Enterprise," in *Innovation*, ed. Rosabeth Moss Kanter, John Kao, and Fred Wiersema (New York: Harper Business, 1997), 43–64.

167 **David Packard ordered them:** David Packard, *The HP Way* (New York: Harper Business, 1995), 108. I also talked with Chuck House about this episode when I first met him at a dinner in 2000, and he was delighted to confirm the story and explain other successes he had at HP because he ignored his misguided superiors and company policies.

167 **"disobedience and its necessity":** Townsend, *Up the Organization*, 28.

171 **Creative incompetence:** Peter and Hull, *The Peter Principle*, 130, 132.

171 **David Friehling:** Diana B. Henriques, "Madoff's Accountant Pleads Guilty in Scheme," *New York Times*, November 3, 2009, http://www.nytimes.com/2009/11/04/business/04madoff.html?_r=1 (accessed November 20, 2009).

174 **Ann Rhoades:** I first reported this incident in Sutton, *The No Asshole Rule*, 70.

174 **his boss gave him a copy:** Bob Sutton, "A Police Officer Uses the No Asshole Rule as a Weapon Against His Boss," Work Matters, September 19, 2008, http://bobsutton.typepad.com/my_weblog/2008/12/a-police-officer-uses-the-no-asshole-rule-as-a-weapon.html (accessed August 25, 2009).

178 **Annette Kyle:** Pfeffer and Sutton, *The Knowing-Doing Gap*, 98–102.

180 **Amazon's most prestigious:** Fred Vogelstein, "Mighty Amazon Jeff Bezos Has Been Hailed as a Visionary and Put Down as a Goofball. He's Proved Critics Wrong by Forging a Winning Management Strategy Built on Brains, Guts, and

Above All, Numbers," *Fortune*, May 26, 2003, http://money.
cnn.com/magazines/fortune/fortune_archive/2003/05/26/
343082/index.htm (accessed August 25, 2009).

Chapter 7

181 **The best bosses don't delay:** Charles A. O'Reilly III and
Barton A. Weitz, "Managing Marginal Employees: The Use of
Warnings and Dismissals," *Administrative Science Quarterly*
25 (1980): 467–484.

183 **Ann Rhoades's history with David Neeleman:** See Jody
Hoffer Gittell and Charles A. O'Reilly III, *JetBlue Airways:
Starting from Scratch*, case no. 801354 (Boston: Harvard
Business School, 2001); and James Wynbrandt, *Flying High*
(New York: Wiley, 2004). The text about Rhoades and
Neeleman was reviewed and corrected via e-mail by Ann
Rhoades on December 4, 2009.

184 **Prediction, Understanding, Control, and Compassion:**
Robert I. Sutton and Robert L. Kahn, "Prediction,
Understanding, and Control as Antidotes to Organizational
Stress," in *Handbook of Organizational Behavior*, ed. Jay
William Lorsch (Englewood Cliffs, NJ: Prentice-Hall, 1987),
272–285; and Pfeffer and Sutton, *The Knowing-Doing Gap*,
136. Many of the ideas in this chapter were published in my
earlier—and more narrowly focused—article: Robert I.
Sutton, "How to Be a Good Boss in a Bad Economy,"
Harvard Business Review 87, no. 6 (2009): 42–50.

184 **safety signal hypothesis:** Martin E. P. Seligman and
Yitzchak M. Binik, "The safety signal hypothesis," in
Operant-Pavlovian Interactions, ed. Hank Davis and Harry
M. B. Hurwitz (Hillsdale, NJ: Lawrence Erlbaum Associates,
1977), 165–187.

185 **surviving multiple rounds of layoffs:** Sarah Moore, Leon
Grunberg, and Edward Greenberg, "Surviving Repeated
Waves of Organizational Downsizing: The Recency,
Duration, and Order Effects Associated with Different Forms

of Layoff Contact," *Anxiety, Stress and Coping* 19 (2006): 309–329.

186 **three thousand Canadian workplaces:** Christopher D. Zatzick and Roderick D. Iverson, "High-Involvement Management and Workforce Reduction: Competitive Advantage or Disadvantage?" *Academy of Management Journal* 49 (2006): 999–1015.

187 **The virtues of careful explanations:** David M. Schweiger and Angelo S. DeNisi, "The Effects of Communication with Employees Following a Merger: A Longitudinal Field Experiment," *Academy of Management Journal* 34 (1991): 117.

188 **The CEO of one software company:** A version of this episode was originally published in Sutton, "How to Be a Good Boss in a Bad Economy."

191 **The worst bosses:** Kelly K. Spors, "If You Fire People, Don't Be a Jerk About It," *Wall Street Journal*, December 29, 2008, http://online.wsj.com/article/SB122981253999624231.html (accessed August 25, 2009); Mike Barry, "Sacking by Text Part of Youth Culture Claims Retailer Blue Banana," Personneltoday.com, August 4, 2006, http://www.personneltoday.com/articles/2006/08/04/36702/sacking-by-text-part-of-youth-culture-claims-retailer-blue-banana.html (accessed August 25, 2009); Associated Press, "RadioShack Layoff Notices Are Sent by E-mail," *New York Times*, August 31, 2006, http://www.nytimes.com/2006/08/31/business/31radio.html (accessed August 25, 2009); and Ieva M. Augstums and Maria Halkias, "RadioShack Lays Off 403 via E-mail," *Dallas Morning News*, August 31, 2006, http://www.dallasnews.com /sharedcontent/dws/bus/stories/083006dnbusradioshack.30c5bc1.html (accessed December 4, 2009).

192 **The damage that clueless:** The report about the insensitive executive was published in Bob Sutton, "Clueless Assholes in Corporate America," Work Matters, December 9, 2006, http://bobsutton.typepad.com/my_weblog/2006/12/

clueless_asshol.html (accessed August 25, 2009). The story concerning Dean Health System is in Dee J. Hall, "Dean Health Nurse Laid Off Mid-Surgery," *Wisconsin State Journal*, April 14, 2009, http://www.madison.com/wsj/mad/latest/446920 (accessed August 25, 2009).

193 **Vice President Ron Thomas:** Carol Hymowitz, "Though Routine, Bosses Still Stumble During the Layoff Process," *Wall Street Journal*, June 26, 2007, http://online.wsj.com/article/SB118272587493646469.html (accessed August 25, 2009).

193 **insomnia among nurses:** Jerald Greenberg, "Losing Sleep over Organizational Injustice: Attenuating Insomniac Reactions to Underpayment Inequity with Supervisory Training in Interactional Justice," *Journal of Applied Psychology* 91 (2006): 63.

194 **Greenberg also shows:** Jerald Greenberg, "Promote Procedural Justice to Enhance Acceptance of Work Outcomes," in *Handbook of Principles of Organizational Behavior*, ed. Edwin A. Locke (Oxford: Blackwell, 2000),189.

195 **CEO Paul Levy:** Kevin Cullen, "A Head with a Heart," *Boston Globe*, March 12, 2009, http://www.boston.com/news/local/massachusetts/articles/2009/03/12/a_head_with_a_heart/ (accessed August 25, 2009).

196 **Research by the management consulting firm Bain:** Darrell Rigby, "Debunking Layoff Myths," from Bain & Company, April 1, 2002, http://www.bain.com/bainweb/publications/publications_detail.asp?id=6759&menu_url=publications_results.asp (accessed August 25, 2009).

197 **Consider a strange program:** Gary P. Latham, "The Importance of Understanding and Changing Employee Outcome Expectancies for Gaining Commitment to an Organizational Goal," *Personnel Psychology* 54, (2001) 707–716.

199 **Research on punishment:** Linda Klebe Trevino, "The Social Effects of Punishment in Organizations: A Justice Perspective," *Academy of Management Review* 17, no. 4 (1992): 647–676.

200 **In a Swedish grocery store:** Ned Carter, Anne Holström, Monica Simpanen, and Lennart Melin, "Theft Reduction in a Grocery Store Through Product Identification and Graphing Losses for Employees," *Journal of Applied Behavior Analysis* 21, no. 4 (1988): 385–389.

200 **Bo Schembechler admitted:** Donald E. Petersen and John Hillkirk, *A Better Idea: Redefining the Way Americans Work* (New York: Houghton Mifflin, 1991), 103–104.

201 **Managers who dish out punishment:** Leanne E. Atwater, Joan F. Bret, and Atira Cherise Charles, "The Delivery of Workplace Discipline: Lessons Learned," *Organizational Dynamics* 36, no. 4 (2007): 392–403.

203 **Research on everything:** Thomas M. Tripp and Robert J. Bies, *Getting Even: The Truth About Workplace Revenge— and How to Stop It* (San Francisco: Jossey-Bass, 2009).

204 **A partner at a large law firm:** Amanda Royal, "Pillsbury Confirms Layoff Leak," *The Recorder*, February 20, 2009; http://www.law.com/jsp/article.jsp?id=1202428436200 (accessed August 11, 2009).

206 **Alice runs Chez Panisse:** Thomas McNamee, *Alice Waters and Chez Panisse: The Romantic, Impractical, Often Eccentric, Ultimately Brilliant Making of a Food Revolution*, (New York: Penguin, 2007), 74.

207 **emotional detachment:** I discuss emotional detachment in my earlier book, *The No Asshole Rule* (New York: Business Plus, 2007); Michael E. McCullough, Kenneth I. Pargament, and Carl E. Thoresen, *Forgiveness: Theory, Research, and Practice* (New York: Guilford Press, 2001).

Chapter 8

210 **A 2007 Zogby survey:** The Workplace Bullying Institute's U.S. Workplace Bullying Survey. http://www. workplacebullying.org/research/WBI-Zogby2007Survey.html (accessed August 10, 2009).

210 **60 percent of workplace incivility:** Christine M. Pearson and Christine Lynne Porath, *The Cost of Bad Behavior: How Incivility Is Damaging Your Business and What to Do About It* (New York: Portfolio, 2009), 15.

210 **2,884 U.S. medical students:** Erica Frank, Jennifer S. Carrera, Terry Stratton, Janet Bickel, and Lois Margaret Nora, "Experiences of Belittlement and Harassment and Their Correlates Among Medical Students in the United States: Longitudinal Survey," *British Medical Journal* 333 (2006): 682–688.

211 **more than 90 percent of nurses:** Laura Sofield and Susan W. Salmond, "Workplace Violence: A Focus on Verbal Abuse and Intent to Leave the Organization." *Orthopaedic Nursing* 22, no. 4 (2003):274–283.

211 **Urban Dictionary:** This definition of bosshole is from http://www.urbandictionary.com/define.php?term=bosshole (accessed August 26, 2009).

211 **ARSE Test:** To take the test, visit http://electricpulp.com/ guykawasaki/arse/ (accessed August 26, 2009).

213 **Evidence of the harm:** Gary Namie and Ruth Namie, *The Bully at Work* (Naperville, IL: Sourcebooks, 2009); Christine M. Pearson and Christine Lynne Porath, *The Cost of Bad Behavior* (New York: Portfolio, 2009); Robert I. Sutton, *The No Asshole Rule* (New York: Business Plus, 2007).

213 **Bossholes make people sick:** Marko Elovainio and others, "Justice at Work and Cardiovascular Mortality: A Prospective Cohort Study," *Journal of Psychosomatic Research* 61, no. 2 (2006): 271–274; Mika Kivimäki and others, "Justice at Work and Reduced Risk of Coronary Heart Disease Among Employees," *Archives of Internal Medicine* 165, no. 19 (2005): 2245–2251; Anna Nyberg and others, "Managerial Leadership and Ischaemic Heart Disease Among Employees: The Swedish WOLF Study," *Occupational and Environmental Medicine* 66 (2009): 51–55.

214 **Certified bossholes:** Sarah J. Tracy, Pamela Lutgen-Sandvik, and Jess K. Alberts, "Nightmares, Demons, and Slaves: Exploring the Painful Metaphors of Workplace Bullying," *Management Communication Quarterly* 20, no. 2 (2006): 148–185.

214 **The collateral damage to loved ones:** Pamela Lutgen-Sandvik, "The Communicative Cycle of Employee Emotional Abuse: Generation and Regeneration of Workplace Mistreatment," *Management Communication Quarterly* 16, no. 4 (2003): 471–501.

214 **When I asked people who read my blog:** The woman who ruined the family dinner and the CEO sent me private e-mails and asked me not to use their names; the victim of the narcissist did leave a public comment. See "The Effects of Asshole Bosses on Victims' Families, Friends, and Partners," Work Matters, July 17, 2009, http://bobsutton.typepad.com/ my_weblog/2009/07/the-effects-of-asshole-bosses-on-victims-familes-friends-and-partners-have-you-suffered-or-seen-coll. html#comments (accessed August 26, 2009).

215 **Bossholes' wicked shenanigans damage performance:** Hochwarter's and Engelhard's survey summarized at Jeanna Bryner, "Abused Workers Fight Back by Slacking Off," *Live Science*, October 8, 2007, http://www.livescience.com/ health/071008-abusive-bosses.html (accessed August 11, 2009); Timothy A. Judge, Brent A. Scott, and Remus Ilies, "Hostility, Job Attitudes, and Workplace Deviance: Test of a Multilevel Model," *Journal of Applied Psychology* 91, no. 1 (2006): 126–138; Judge quote from "Even Good Employees Act Up If Supervisors Mistreat Them," Newswise, April 26, 2006, http://www.newswise.com/articles/view/519447/ (accessed August 26, 2009); James R. Detert and others, "Managerial Modes of Influence and Counterproductivity in Organizations: A Longitudinal Business-Unit-Level Investigation," *Journal of Applied Psychology* 92, no. 4 (2007): 993–1005.

216 **Imagine the effect on customers:** Karl Vick, "Team-Building or Torture? Court Will Decide," *Washington Post*, April 13, 2008, http://www.washingtonpost.com/wp-dyn/content/article/2008/04/12/AR2008041201739.html (accessed August 26, 2009).

217 **Although the suit was dismissed:** Jeremy Duda, "Judge Dismisses Waterboarding Lawsuit," *Daily Herald*, Utah, August 5, 2008, http://www.heraldextra.com/news/local/article_95ac550b-526a-527e-8713-56a2cb897b00.html (accessed December 4, 2009).

218 **"Asshole taxes":** "Evidence-Based 'Asshole Pricing' at a UK Consulting Firm," Work Matters, September 27, 2007, http://bobsutton.typepad.com/my_weblog/2007/09/evidence-based-.html (accessed August 26, 2009).

218 **Bossholes also generate legal costs:** *Daniel H. Raess, M.D. vs. Joseph E. Doescher*, Indiana Supreme Court, No. 49S02-0710-CV-424, filed April 8, 2008, www.in.gov/judiciary/opinions/pdf/04080801bd.pdf (accessed August 26, 2009).

219 **At least seventeen states:** See the Healthy Workplace Bill website for information about legislation that is being considered and has been passed in various states, http://healthyworkplacebill.org/ (accessed December 4, 2009).

219 **self-inflicted wounds:** Pamela Lutgen-Sandvik, "Take This Job and...: Quitting and Other Forms of Resistance to Workplace Bullying," *Communication Monographs* 73, (2006): 406–433.

220 **Professor Dacher Keltner:** Dacher Keltner, "The Power Paradox," *Greater Good* IV, no. 3 (Winter 2007–2008): 14–17; Also see Gerben A. Van Kleef and others, "Power, Distress, and Compassion: Turning a Blind Eye to the Suffering of Others," *Psychological Science* 19, no. 12 (2008): 1315–1322.

221 **subordinates are hypervigilant:** Susan T. Fiske, "Controlling Other People: The Impact of Power on Stereotyping," *American Psychologist* 48, no. 6 (1993): 621–628; Dacher Keltner, Debora H. Gruenfeld, and Cameron Anderson,

"Power, Approach, and Inhibition," *Psychological Review* 110, no. 2 (2003): 265–284.

222 **Similar insensitivity:** "There Apparently Isn't a No Asshole Rule," She's Lump, March 18, 2009, http://newkate.blogspot. com/2009/03/there-apparently-isnt-no-asshole-rule.html (accessed August 26, 2008).

223 **Employee Max Goldman explained:** "SuccessFactors: 'My Boss Thanked Me for Calling Him a Jerk,'" Work Matters, February 7, 2007, http://bobsutton.typepad.com/my_ weblog/2007/02/successfactors_.html (accessed August 26, 2008).

225 **Time pressure:** Christine M. Pearson and Christine Lynne Porath, *The Cost of Bad Behavior* (New York: Portfolio, 2009); John M. Darley and C. Daniel Batson, "From Jerusalem to Jericho: A Study of Situational and Dispositional Variables in Helping Behavior," *Journal of Personality and Social Psychology* 27, no. 1 (1973): 100–108.

227 **Winston Churchill:** Joseph Cardieri, "Churchill Understood Afternoon Naps," *New York Times*, October 2, 1989, http://www.nytimes.com/1989/10/02/opinion/l-churchill-understood-afternoon-naps-838589.html (accessed August 26, 2009).

228 **Research on sleep deprivation:** Yvonne Harrison and James A. Horne, "The Impact of Sleep Deprivation on Decision Making: A Review," *Journal of Experimental Psychology, Applied* 6, no. 3 (2000): 236–249; Heather Hatfield, "The Power of Napping," http://www.webmd.com/ sleep-disorders/features/power-of-napping-feature (accessed October 14, 2009); Suzanne R. Daiss, Amy D. Bertelson, and Ludy T. Benjamin, Jr., "Napping vs. Resting: Effects on Performance and Mood," *Psychophysiology* 23, no. 1 (1986): 82–88; Brian Wiegand, "Is It Nap Time Yet?," Flywheel, September 12, 2008, http://flywheelblog. com/2008/09/is-it-nap-time-yet/ (accessed August 26, 2008).

229 **Shakespeare got it right:** Craig A. Anderson, "Temperature and Aggression: Ubiquitous Effects of Heat on Occurrence of Human Violence," *Psychological Bulletin* 106, no. 1 (1989): 74–96; Alan S. Reifman, Richard P. Larrick, and Steven Fein, "Temper and Temperature on the Diamond: The Heat-Aggression Relationship in Major League Baseball," *Personality and Social Psychology Bulletin* 17, no. 5 (1991): 580–585.

230 **Scott Berkun suggests:** Scott Berkun, "Top Ten Reasons Managers Become Assholes," the Berkun Blog, January 19, 2009, http://www.scottberkun.com/blog/2009/top-ten-reasons-managers-become-assholes/ (accessed August 26, 2009).

231 **A head surgeon:** Robert Sutton, "Breaking the cycle of abuse in medicine," Work Matters, March 13, 2007, http://bobsutton.typepad.com/my_weblog/2007/03/breaking_the_cy.html (accessed August 26, 2009).

232 **Emotions are remarkably contagious:** Elaine Hatfield, John T. Cacioppo, and Richard L. Rapson, *Emotional Contagion* (Cambridge: Cambridge University Press, 1993).

233 **One of the most popular postings:** Robert Sutton, "Marge's Asshole Management Metric: Update," Work Matters, September 8, 2007, http://bobsutton.typepad.com/my_weblog/2007/03/marges_asshole_.html (accessed August 26, 2009).

236 **Embarrassment and pride:** Sociologists have long argued that these are potent motivators of human behavior. See, for example, Erving Goffman, *The Presentation of Self in Everyday Life* (New York: Doubleday, 1959).

Chapter 9

244 **David Dunning, of Cornell University:** David Dunning, *Self-Insight* (New York: Psychology Press, 2005).

245 **Former GE CEO Jack Welch:** Robert Joss, "It's Not About You," *Stanford GSB News*, August 2007, http://www.gsb.

stanford.edu/news/research/joss_you.html (accessed
September 3, 2009).

246 **Linda Hudson learned:** Adam Bryant, "Corner Office: Fitting
In, and Rising to the Top," *New York Times*, September 19,
2009, http://www.nytimes.com/2009/09/20/business/
20corner.html?_r=3&scp=2&sq=scarf%20CEO&st=cse
(accessed October 13, 2009).

246 **Intel executive Patricia "Pat" McDonald:** This story
emerged through a series of e-mail exchanges that I had
with Intel's Sumit Guha, Pat McDonald, Bill Mackenzie, and
Matt Brownfield between October 7 and October 15 in 2009.

INDEX

ABOUT THE AUTHOR

Robert Sutton is Professor of Management Science and Engineering at Stanford and a Professor of Organizational Behavior, by courtesy, at the Stanford Graduate School of Business. Sutton studies leaders and bosses, innovation, evidence-based management, and the nitty-gritty of organizational life. His books include *Weird Ideas That Work: How to Build a Creative Company*, *The Knowing-Doing Gap: How Smart Companies Turn Knowledge into Action* (with Jeffrey Pfeffer), *Hard Facts, Dangerous Half-Truths, and Total Nonsense: Profiting from Evidence-Based Management* (also with Jeffrey Pfeffer), and the *New York Times* and *BusinessWeek* bestseller *The No Asshole Rule: Building a Civilized Workplace and Surviving One That Isn't*. *The No Asshole Rule* has been translated into 19 languages; these non-English editions have sold over 350,000 copies.

Professor Sutton's honors include the award for the best paper published in the *Academy of Management Journal* in 1989, the Eugene L. Grant Award for Excellence in Teaching, selection by *Business 2.0* as a leading "management guru" in 2002, and the award for the best article published in the *Academy of Management Review* in 2005. *Hard Facts, Dangerous Half-Truths, and Total Nonsense* was selected as the best business book of 2006 by the *Toronto Globe and Mail,* and *The No Asshole Rule* won the Quill Award for the best business book of 2007. Sutton was named as one of 10 "B-School All-Stars" by *BusinessWeek* in 2007, which they described as "professors who are influencing contemporary business thinking far beyond academia." Sutton has given speeches and run workshops for executives and managers in dozens of industries from over 25 different countries. Especially dear to his heart is the Hasso Plattner Institute of Design, which everyone calls "the Stanford d.school." He is a co-founder of this multidisciplinary program, which teaches, practices, and spreads "design thinking." His personal blog is Work Matters, at www.bobsutton.net.

Also by Robert I. Sutton

*The Knowing-Doing Gap: How Smart Companies Turn
     Knowledge Into Action* (1999, with Jeffrey Pfeffer)
*Weird Ideas That Work: How to Build a Creative
     Company* (2002)
*Hard Facts, Dangerous Half-Truths, and Total Nonsense:
     Profiting from Evidence-Based Management* (2006,
     with Jeffrey Pfeffer)
*The No Asshole Rule: Building a Civilized Workplace and
     Surviving One That Isn't* (2007)

**BUSINESS
PLUS**

Recognized as one of the world's most prestigious business imprints, Business Plus specializes in publishing books that are on the cutting edge. Like you, to be successful we always strive to be ahead of the curve.

Business Plus titles encompass a wide range of books and interests—including important business management works, state-of-the-art personal financial advice, noteworthy narrative accounts, the latest in sales and marketing advice, individualized career guidance, and autobiographies of the key business leaders of our time.

Our philosophy is that business is truly global in every way, and that today's business reader is looking for books that are both entertaining and educational. To find out more about what we're publishing, please check out the Business Plus blog at:

www.businessplusblog.com